DRIED FLOWERS

DRIED FLOWERS

An inspirational guide to drying flowers and plants for decoration and scent around the home.

PENNY BLACK

CAVENDISH BOOKS

VANCOUVER

First published in Great Britain in 1994 by Covent Garden Books,
9 Henrietta Street, London WC2E 8PS

This edition published in Canada by Cavendish Books Inc.,
Unit 5, 801 West 1st Street,
North Vancouver, B.C. V7P 1A4

Canadian Cataloguing in Publication Data
Black, Penny.
Dried Flowers
Includes index.
ISBN 0-929050-44-4
1. Dried flower arrangement. 2. Flower-Drying.
3. Potpourris (Scented floral mixtures) I. Title.
SB449.3.D7B57 1995   745.92   C95-910395-3

ISBN 0-929050-44-4

Printed and bound in Spain by Graficromo

~Contents~

Pressed Flowers

My involvement in the art of pressed flowers stems from my lifelong love affair with flowers and gardening. My very first memories are of catching hold of my mother's hand and wandering into a bleak winter garden to look at the little green spears of snowdrops pushing through the frozen soil. Very early on I began to explore the woods, meadows and hedgerows that surrounded our little thatched cottage.

Flowers were everywhere and my year began with snowdrops and primroses, followed by an exciting search for the stinking hellebore, and then the daffodils, wood anemones, violets, campions, ragged-robins, bluebells, dog's mercury, orchids and spurge arrived. In those days I picked them all and they were crammed into jam jars with no thought of artistic arrangement. Surprisingly, as a child I did not press any flowers. In fact I did not start pressing flowers at all until well into adult life. I had started making and selling perfumed sachets, to earn some money, but with so many people around with the same idea, I felt that to succeed I must come up with something original. Then I had the idea of decorating lace-edged calico sachets with little pressed rosebuds.

However, my thoughts were always turning to pressed flower collages where I felt there was tremendous scope. In my mind's eye I could vaguely see what I wanted to do but could never put it into practice. I made plenty of stylized flower pictures but was never happy with them. I wanted to capture the abundance of my garden, and the thin collages that I was making did nothing to convey this image. Then, a few years ago, in what must have been a moment of lateral inspiration, I made my first jumbled attempt at a "Wild Garden" picture and knew that I was on the right path; I could actually see my garden in it and with a few more attempts I felt confident enough to submit one for an exhibition. One idea led to another and I realized that there were endless possibilities.

I hope this section will inspire you to experiment with pressing flowers. Not only will you gain immense satisfaction and pleasure from creating flower pictures, but you will also deepen your knowledge of plants and gardening and develop a greater appreciation for our beautiful countryside.

Plant
Material

*Wherever you live, whether in
the town, in the country, or by the sea,
there is a wide range of flowers,
leaves, mosses, lichens, ferns,
seedheads, and even fruit and vegetables
that you can gather and press for your flower pictures.
The following pages show the different
kinds of plant material available,
but be careful: never pick protected or endangered
plants from the wild.*

~Gathering Plant Material~

There is a wealth of plant material you can gather for pressing. Don't limit yourself solely to flowers that grow in your garden, but search woodlands and hedgerows, beaches and meadows, where there are lots of unusual things you can press: spiralling stalks; green flowers and silky seedheads; seeds and flowers from trees; and unusual seaweeds. Don't forget ponds and streams either, where you will find water fern, parrot weed and other pond plants. And, of course, grasses and rushes, mosses, lichens and fungi can all be pressed very successfully to create unusual combinations of textures, shapes and colours.

Conserving Plants

When gathering wild plants only pick as much as you need. Remember that it is against the law to pick or uproot any rare wild plant (see page 160 for a conservation list of protected plants). The same applies to the flowers you grow in your garden; there is no point pressing your rarest specimen, and neither should you strip plants of all their blossoms, buds or leaves.

Plant material should be quite dry when you gather it; the early afternoon is the ideal gathering time. Give the flowers a sharp nudge before picking them, if hidden water droplets are jerked out, this means a few more hours of drying are necessary. Select only undamaged, fresh blossoms and leaves, as faded, stale plant material will not improve with pressing. And the sooner you can press your gathered plants, the better the finished results will be.

Flower border
(right)
A summer border is the ideal place to gather flowers for pressing. Here dusky pink scabious, dwarf purple larkspur and oxeye daisies are all ripe for picking.

Shady corner
(below)
Growing wild in this shady patch are rosebay willowherb, crane's-bill and hogweed, all of which press beautifully.

~Gathering & Preparation~

When gathering plant material for pressing, take only as much as you need. Try to leave behind plenty of buds and flowers, especially when gathering from the wild. In fact it is against the law to pick or uproot any rare wild plant (see page 160 for more details on conservation). You can try gathering a little of everything to begin with – single blossoms, sprays, leaves, buds, seedheads, and even the occasional plant complete with roots. Try the unexpected: stinging nettles, iris and lily petals, trailing wands of climbing plants, and bunches of newly formed grapes.

Flowers should be at their best when you pick them, when their colours are richest. This is usually when they have just opened, not when they have been flowering for some time. The petals should be clean, undamaged and fresh. It is important to gather your plant material on a dry day as dampness encourages mildew; the afternoon is best as any morning dew will have evaporated by then. In an absolute emergency, however, wet flowers can be picked and left to dry in a vase of water indoors.

When you are collecting plant material, put the specimens in a polythene bag to keep them fresh. Don't overfill the bag, though, in case the flowers crush each other. Before you seal the bag, blow air into it and then secure the open end with a plastic tie. This air pocket prevents the flowers from becoming crushed, dried out or too hot. If the flowers have wilted by the time you get home, put the polythene bag with its contents in the fridge or a cool place until they perk up again.

Plant material should be pressed as soon as possible after it has been picked, to retain its colour, but some preparation will be required first. When handling single blossoms and delicate buds, use forceps or tweezers to avoid damaging the petals.

Preparing Different Blossoms

Single blossoms, such as potentilla and meadow buttercup, press flat very easily, with or without their stalks. Cut the stalks off with sharp scissors if you do not want them. Sprays of flowers, such as hydrangea or forget-me-not, can be pressed whole or separated into individual blooms. Use sharp scissors to cut off each bloom, being very careful not to damage the petals.

Some double flowers benefit from being thinned out. Cut the flower-head off the stalk, then carefully pluck out a few of the central petals, to make a flatter flower-head. Three-dimensional flowers, such as rosebuds and daffodils,

Slicing flower-heads

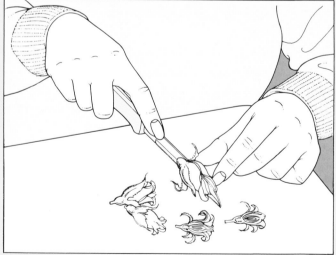

Slice bulky, three-dimensional flower-heads, such as rosebuds and daffodils, in half lengthways before pressing them. To do this, hold the flower-head steady on a table and carefully cut through it, from the tip to the base, with a sharp knife. Both halves of the flower-head can then be used, and since each half has a flat surface, this makes it easier to glue them on to the flower picture.

Preparing vegetables

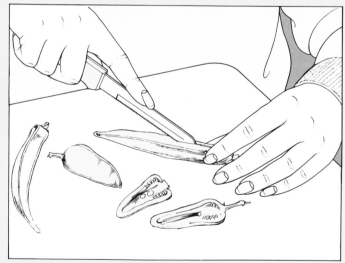

Slice long, thin vegetables, such as okra and chilli peppers, either lengthways or widthways before pressing them. To do this, hold the vegetable steady on a table, between finger and thumb, and then slice through it with a sharp knife, drawing the knife away from your hand. Remove any stray seeds or strands of vegetable skin, and blot any juicy or wet areas with a tissue.

can be cut in half lengthways with scissors or a scalpel, before being pressed. You can then use both halves in your picture. Alternatively, you can press the flower whole for a more textured effect. You will need to make a "collar" (see the illustration) for flowers that have thick centres, to keep the petals pressed flat, without unduly squashing the flower centre, when pressing the flower.

Unusual Plant Material

If you are unable to obtain some flowers, you can always use *dried flowers*. Before pressing them, hold them in the steam from a kettle to revitalize them.

Most *lichens*, *mosses* and *barks* need not be pressed. I arrange them on a tray and leave them in a warm, dry spot for a day or so, by which time they will be ready for use. If the material is not flat enough for use then a few hours in a press will flatten them, but I think that half the beauty of this plant material is its texture.

Tiny *toadstools* do not need any preparation before pressing, but larger *fungi* can be cut in half lengthways, or into cross-sections, before being pressed lightly. I only press material that I can positively identify as being non-poisonous. Before pressing segments of *seaweed*, wash them thoroughly in tap water to remove the salty sea water and then dab them dry with tissues.

Fruit and *vegetables*, such as beans, chillies, okra, peppers and most soft fruit, can be cut in half lengthways, or into cross-sections, before being pressed. You can remove the fruit skin or rind and press this separately.

Steaming dried flowers

Hold dried flowers in the steam from a boiling kettle for a minute or so before pressing them. The moist steam will revitalize the flowers. Be careful not to scald yourself; it is best to steam only long-stemmed flowers, so that your hands are kept out of the steam.

Making a collar

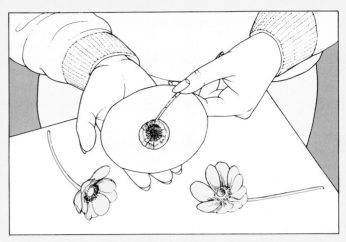

To make a flower collar, cut out a piece of blotting paper the size of the flower-head. Cut a hole in the middle of this the same size as the bulky centre. Place this collar over the flower so the flower centre protrudes through the hole. Add further collars until the top of the flower centre is level with the top layer of collars.

Thinning sprays of flowers

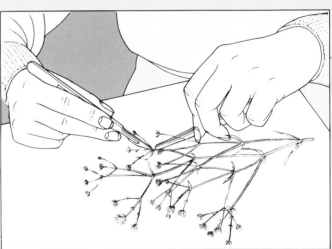

Sprays of flowers, such as lady's-mantle and baby's breath may require thinning before they are pressed. Using tweezers or forceps to avoid crushing the flowers, hold the spray steady on a flat surface. With a scalpel carefully slice off smaller stalks throughout the spray where necessary. You can use scissors instead of a scalpel if you prefer, though the results may not be as neat.

~ Effects of Pressing ~

The most obvious effect of pressing a flower is that it becomes flat and two-dimensional. This immediately alters the whole appearance, shape and size of the plant. Small flowers appear larger when their petals are flattened and spread out, and subtle colours and shapes of petals and leaves become more apparent. You can see different aspects of a flower for the first time, such as the lovely pink flower centres of hellebores and the delicate striping of the undersides of astrantia petals.

Colour Changes

The colours of pressed flowers can also change dramatically. If you compare any freshly picked flower with its pressed counterpart, the two flowers never have exactly the same hue. Many colours acquire more depth and luxury after pressing. Any red flowers that press well, such as roses and anemones, will always become richer and darker and there will also be a touch of blue in their colour. Blue flowers, too, become more intense after pressing. Orange and yellow flowers, such as potentilla, tend to become a shade darker, while green leaves and petals are very variable: some become a richer green whilst some barely change at all. White flowers can often turn the colour of parchment, though very quick drying and pressing can sometimes produce a good white. If you come across some plant material that does not press well and turns brown, don't discard it — instead, mix it with other flowers in a "random" flower collage.

The change in some plants can be startling. Wood cow-wheat and lady's bedstraw, for example, often turn black when pressed and as such can look particularly striking in a flower collage. Another example is Cape marigold, the pink star of the veldt, that turns a beautiful dove grey when pressed. Most red and blue primroses turn a uniform shade of heliotrope, with the exception of the gold-laced and Cowichan polyanthuses which often turn velvety black. If you keep experimenting with pressing different flowers, you will learn which plants press well and produce the most interesting and rewarding results.

Pressed cow parsley

Fresh cow parsley

Pressed anemones

Fresh anemones

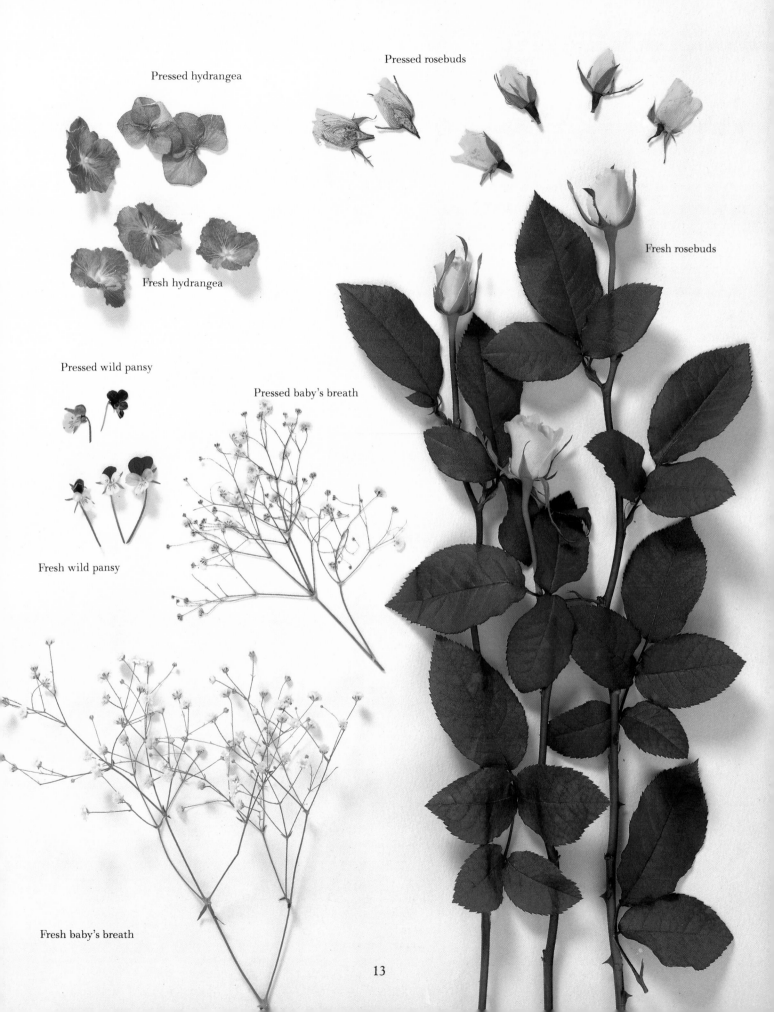

Pressed hydrangea

Pressed rosebuds

Fresh rosebuds

Fresh hydrangea

Pressed wild pansy

Pressed baby's breath

Fresh wild pansy

Fresh baby's breath

13

~The Garden~

The garden is a rich source of colour, providing an abundance of flowers and leaves for pressing all through the year. The striking pinks and reds of old rose blossoms compete with rich purple crane's-bills, scarlet fuchsias and sunny yellow daffodils; while the pale pastel colours of pink and cream anemones, astrantias and Cape marigolds soften and subdue brighter colours.

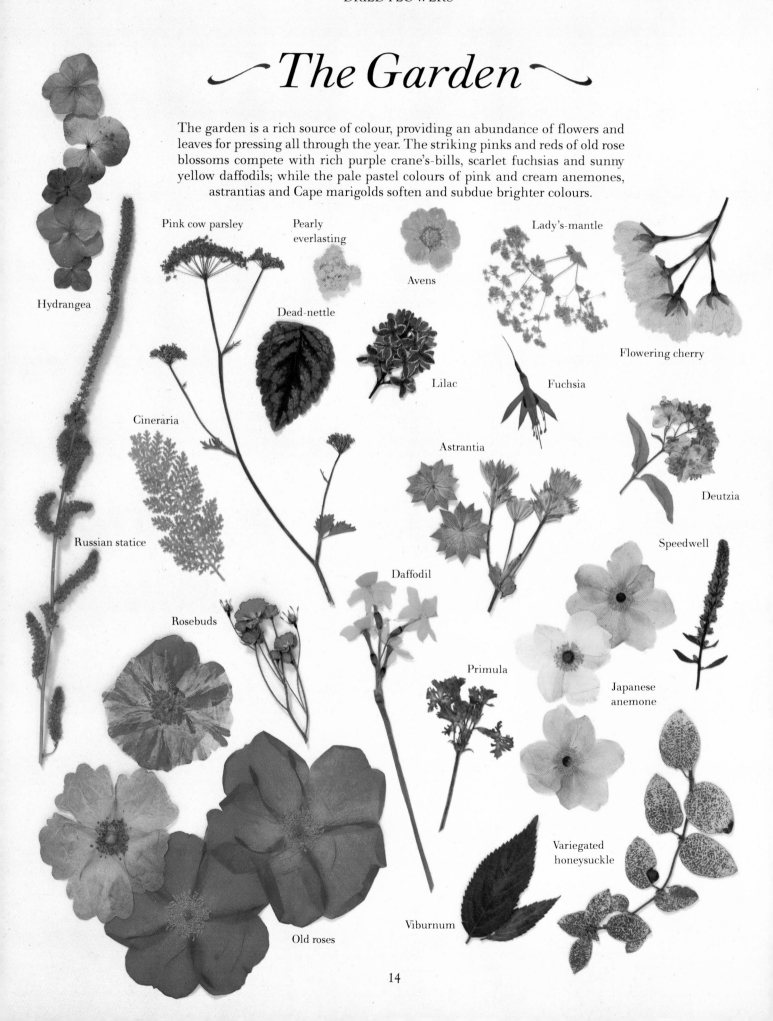

Hydrangea

Pink cow parsley

Pearly everlasting

Avens

Lady's-mantle

Flowering cherry

Dead-nettle

Lilac

Fuchsia

Cineraria

Astrantia

Deutzia

Russian statice

Speedwell

Daffodil

Rosebuds

Primula

Japanese anemone

Variegated honeysuckle

Viburnum

Old roses

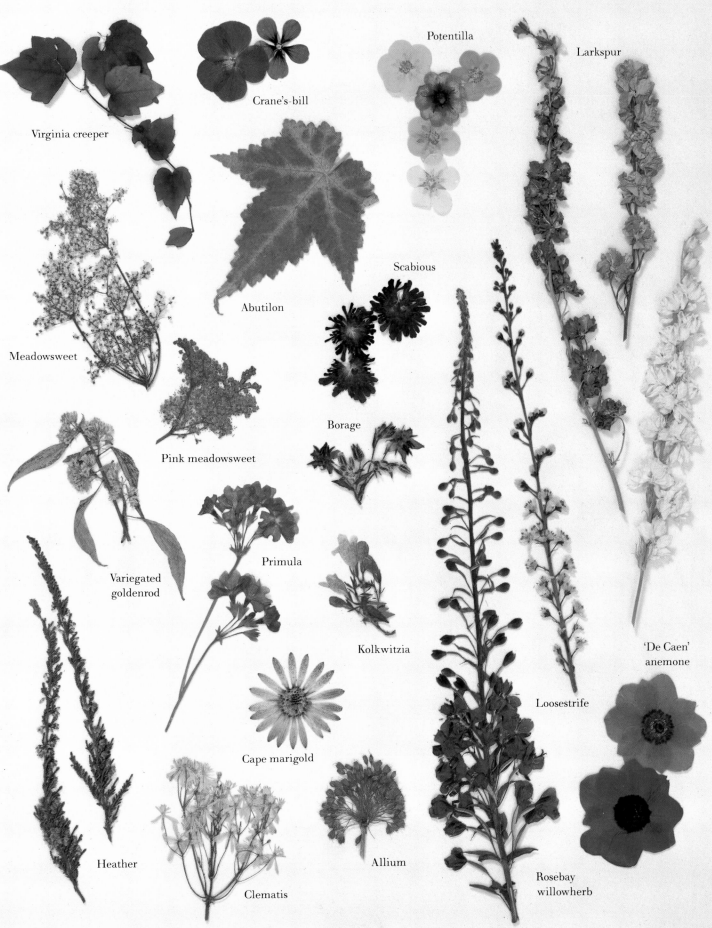

Virginia creeper

Crane's-bill

Potentilla

Larkspur

Abutilon

Scabious

Meadowsweet

Pink meadowsweet

Borage

Variegated
goldenrod

Primula

Kolkwitzia

'De Caen'
anemone

Cape marigold

Loosestrife

Heather

Clematis

Allium

Rosebay
willowherb

~The Hedgerow~

Hedgerows are a rich source of plant material that you can press. There are colourful and pretty celandine and red campion flower-heads, long spiky stems of burnet and pussy willow, and fluffy seedheads of traveller's-joy, while the tiny umbels of cow parsley and hemlock water-dropwort are invaluable for softening edges in your flower pictures.

Dock

Honesty

Hazel catkins

Wormwood

Hemlock water-dropwort

Celandine

Cow parsley

Wood woundwort

Stitchwort

Burnet

Comfrey

Strawberry

Celandine

White common dog-violet

Pussy willow

Blackberry

Crosswort

Hop

Yarrow

Climbing fumitory

Common knapweed

Common horsetail

Rat-tailed plantain

Ivy-leaved toadflax

Red campion

Sorrel

Periwinkle

Bitter vetch

Rough chervil

Hazel catkins

Wood sage

Traveller's-joy

Wall fumitory

Rosebay willowherb

~ The Woodland ~

The cool, dappled shade cast by trees in a wood provides a home for many lovely woodland plants. In the spring there are carpets of bluebells and yellow-green spurge, and if you search carefully you will find dainty wood anemones, violets, snowdrops and primroses. Later in the year you can collect all sorts of catkins, berries, seedheads and skeletonized leaves to press.

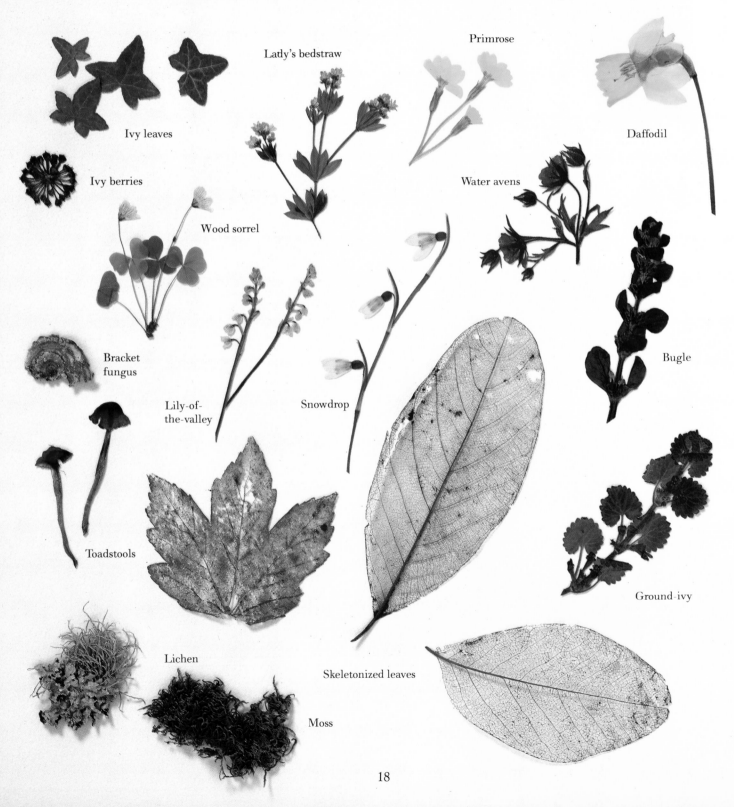

Ivy leaves

Ivy berries

Lady's bedstraw

Primrose

Daffodil

Wood sorrel

Water avens

Bracket fungus

Bugle

Lily-of-the-valley

Snowdrop

Toadstools

Ground-ivy

Lichen

Skeletonized leaves

Moss

Alder catkins

Wood spurge

Spurge

Great wood-rush

Dusky crane's-bill

Bluebells

Hard shield fern fronds

Sycamore flowers

White bluebells

Broad buckler fern

Maidenhair spleenwort

Hart's-tongue fern fronds

Wood violet

Wood anemones

Wood forget-me-not

~ The Meadow ~

The sight of a wildflower meadow full of colourful flowers immediately fills me with nostalgia. Many of my favourite flowers of childhood thrive in meadow pastures – buttercups, daisies, cowslips and cuckooflowers, all of which press beautifully. But be sensible when picking your flowers; always leave plenty behind to set seed and never pick any rare wild flowers.

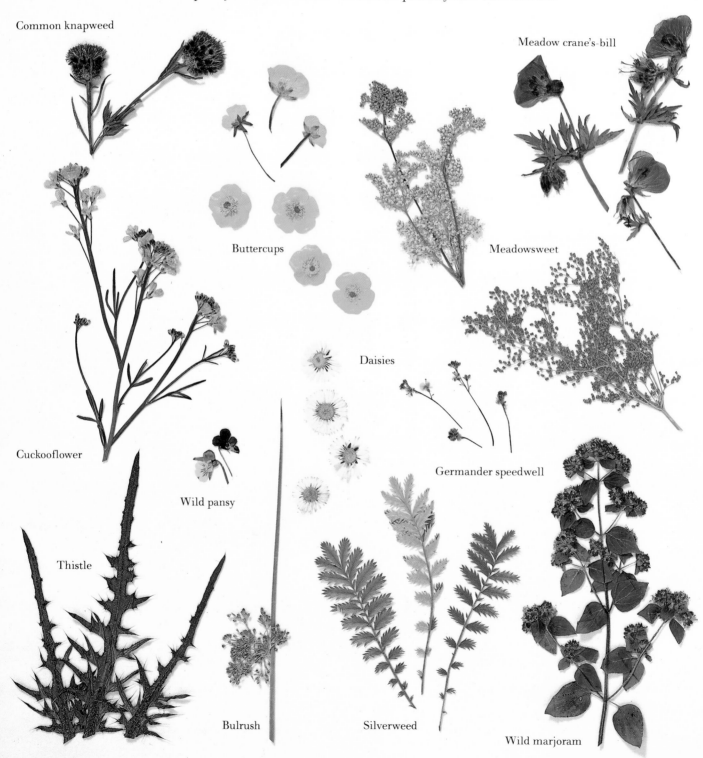

Common knapweed

Meadow crane's-bill

Buttercups

Meadowsweet

Cuckooflower

Daisies

Germander speedwell

Wild pansy

Thistle

Bulrush

Silverweed

Wild marjoram

Cowslips

Red clover

Cow parsley

Bird's-foot-trefoil

Plantain

Sorrel

Marsh-marigold

Various grasses

～Ferns～

There is a wonderful range of ferns and fern-like leaves you can press and use in your flower pictures, from the light and delicate asparagus fern to the bold and dramatic hart's tongue fern. Ferns are calm and restful, conveying a suggestion of shady glades. The more feathery ferns soften a picture and make pretty lacy patterns, while the thicker and heavier ferns create a bolder image.

Shuttlecock fern

Hard fern

Leather fern

Hard shield
fern frond

Beech fern

Maidenhair
spleenwort

Crested
polypody

Black spleenwort

Mature hard
shield fern

Young hard
shield fern

Asparagus fern

Bracken

Common polypody

Sweet cicely

Crested buckler fern

Hart's tongue

Maidenhair fern

Common horsetail

~Seedheads~

There is a tremendous variety of seedheads available for pressing and drying. Some have fascinating shapes, such as the circular-shaped sea carrot and the bearded traveller's-joy, while the knobbly clusters of rose hips and blackberries provide interesting textures. Other seedheads have an unusual beauty, such as the pearly seed-cases of honesty. As most seedheads are in neutral tones of brown and green, they can be used in most compositions.

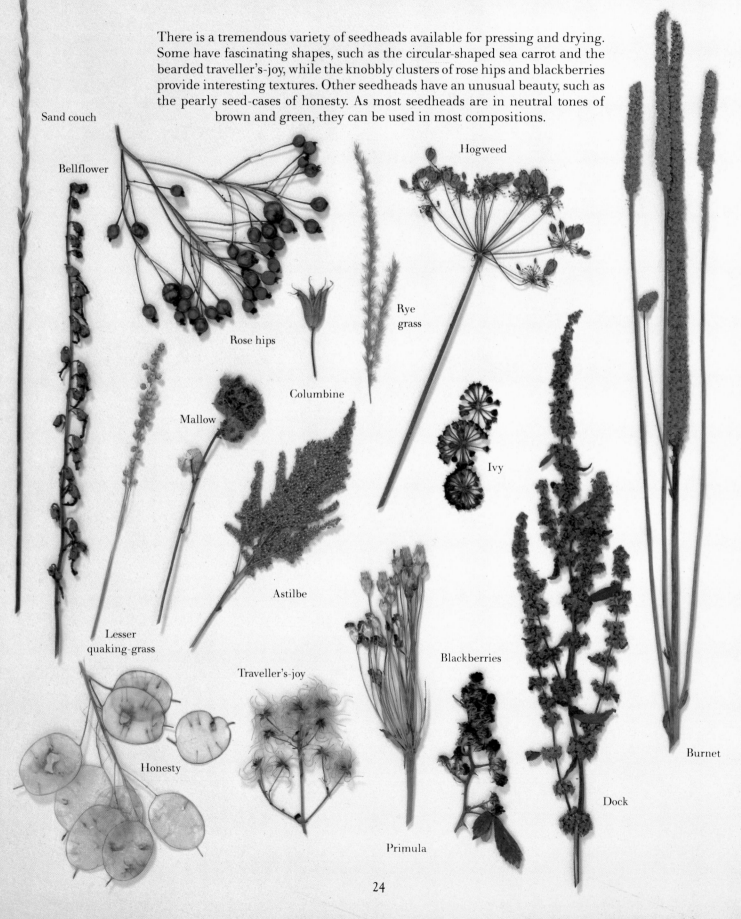

Sand couch

Bellflower

Hogweed

Rose hips

Rye grass

Columbine

Mallow

Ivy

Astilbe

Lesser quaking-grass

Blackberries

Traveller's-joy

Burnet

Honesty

Dock

Primula

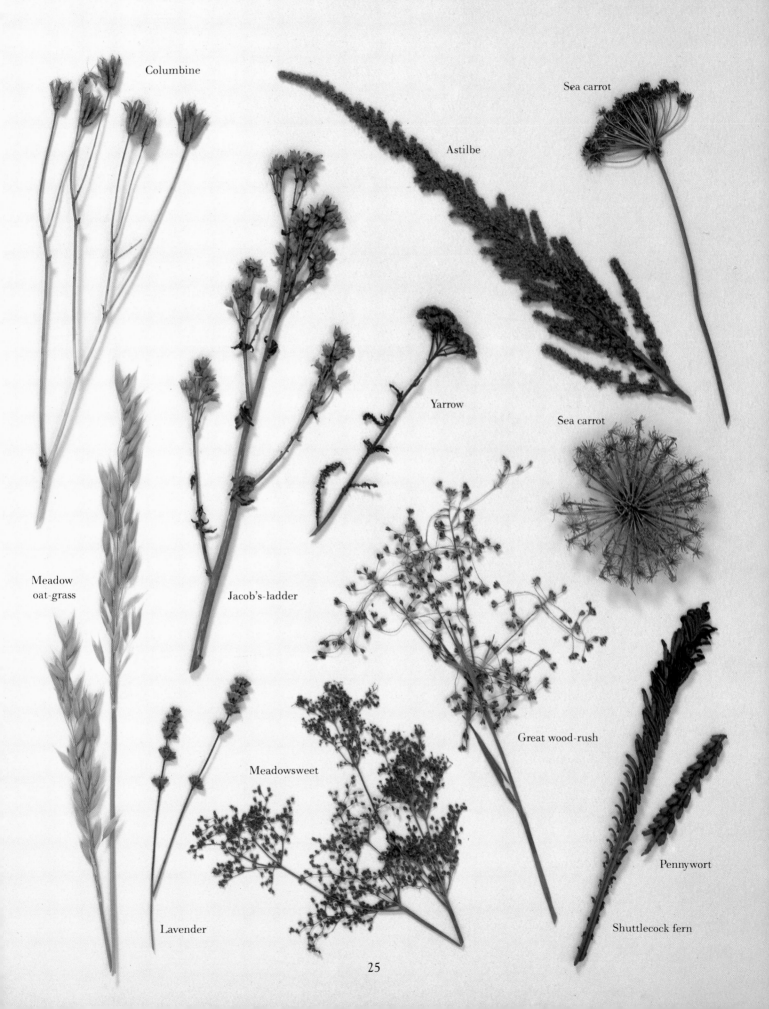

Columbine

Astilbe

Sea carrot

Yarrow

Sea carrot

Meadow
oat-grass

Jacob's-ladder

Great wood-rush

Meadowsweet

Pennywort

Lavender

Shuttlecock fern

25

~ Leaves & Bark ~

Skeletonized leaves are invaluable for my flower pictures and they are not hard to find; I collected the specimens below during a walk through the woods. I use them to form the base layer of my pictures; their intricate veining makes delicate, lacy patterns subduing and softening the colour beneath. Tree bark is useful as its coarse texture adds interest and depth to a picture.

Oak

Holly

Eryngium

Maple

Magnolia

Tree bark

Materials
& Techniques

*The following pages show the
essential tools and equipment you will need
for making pressed flower pictures,
including cutting implements, papers and boards,
fabrics and writing tools.
The techniques to use are simple and straightforward;
with a little practice, you will quickly master
them and be able to set to work
creating your own flower collages.*

~Tools & Equipment~

The most essential tool I have is an old pair of forceps, with which I handle all my plant material. You may prefer to use tweezers, but I find them a little clumsy.

The other basic items of equipment are: rubber-based glue, orange sticks to apply it, pencils, a rubber and a ruler, French curves to draw round, a sharp knife to cut straight edges, hair spray to fix plant material on completed collages, and a pair of sharp scissors. Many other items are useful but not vital.

The ultimate indulgence, however, would be a room of your own to work in. For years I have worked in the kitchen, on the one and only work surface, surrounded by family and animals, cups of tea and toasted cheese sandwiches. We have all survived quite happily, but what bliss to have a room of one's own!

Scalpel

Small nail scissors

Sharp craft knife

Soft brush

Putty rubber

Blunt-edged
tweezers

Forceps

Soft rubbers

Large scissors

Masking tape

Metal ruler

Clear plastic ruler

Soft 2B
pencil

Clear glue

Rubber-based glue

Saucer of rubber-based glue

Tissue

One-way nappy liner

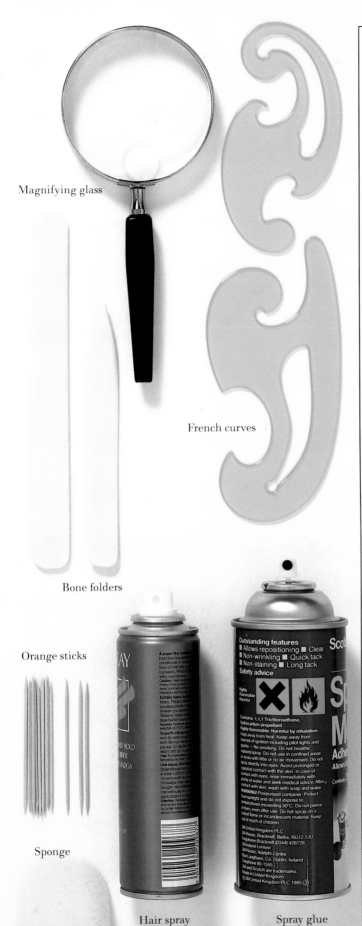

Magnifying glass

French curves

Bone folders

Orange sticks

Sponge

Hair spray

Spray glue

FLOWER PRESSES

Although you may start by using a magazine or heavy book in which to press your flowers and leaves, a flower press does give better results and is essential for those wanting to take the craft seriously. There are several different types and sizes of press available. Two examples are illustrated below.

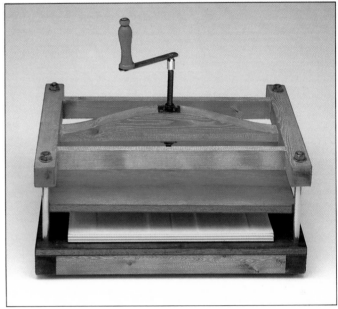

Professional press

This is a heavy-duty professional press which is ideal for those who are serious about flower pressing. With only one central screw it is easy and quick to operate. It can also take a lot of pressure, making it useful for pressing very bulky and textured plant material.

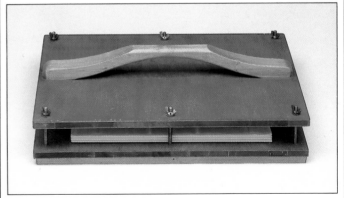

Simple press

This press is lighter and more manageable than the professional press though the pressure it applies is not as great. However, it is perfectly adequate as a general press for flowers and leaves and less textured plant material. It operates by tightening six wing nuts and bolts.

~ *Flower Presses* ~

If you have never pressed any flowers before, you may feel a little unsure as to which press to start off with. It certainly need not be anything too elaborate: for a couple of years I used only a makeshift press, consisting of two pieces of plywood and three bricks! From this, I progressed on to a good homemade working press, and it has only been in the last year that I have had my professional, heavy-duty press. Of course, this is the best type of press to use, but it is not necessary in the beginning.

Choosing a Press

It is possible to press flowers in a magazine or book as a temporary measure. To apply pressure, put a heavy weight on top, or else insert the magazine or book under the carpet in a spot where there is a lot of coming and going, or under the cushion of a well-used chair: necessity must be the mother of invention! However, I would only recommend this in an emergency, when you have nothing else you can use. A makeshift press is a good press to start off with. It is very cheap to make; all you need are two spare pieces of plywood and some heavy weights such as bricks. Place your material to be pressed in between tissues or one-way nappy liners and place these between sheets of absorbent paper (the illustration opposite shows

a breakdown of the layers of paper to use). Then sandwich all these layers between your pieces of plywood and place three bricks or similar heavy weights on top. This type of press has the advantage of maintaining constant pressure whilst the flowers and leaves dry out. Other presses have to be tightened continually.

If you are prepared to spend some money on a more advanced press, you should consider progressing on to a simple, traditional press. You can either buy one or make one. A traditional press usually works by tightening four wing nuts and bolts, one at each corner of the press, which slowly presses the plant material that is sandwiched in layers of paper in the middle.

Then, if you find you want a stronger press, you can't do better than a heavy-duty professional press. You can press absolutely anything in one of these presses, including very bulky and textured plant material, which of course gives you a greater variety of material to work with. The professional press works by a central screw, and is less bothersome to use than four wing nuts and bolts of a traditional press.

Always make sure that your presses are stored in a dry place with a good circulation of air, to guard against damp and mildew, the arch enemies of pressed flowers.

Makeshift press

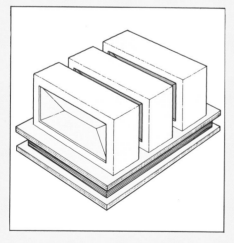

This is an excellent press for a beginner. You need two pieces of plywood and three bricks. Place your flowers between layers of absorbent paper (see the illustration opposite) and sandwich these between the pieces of plywood. Then place the bricks on top.

Travelling press

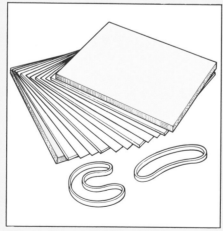

This is ideal for carrying with you when you are gathering flowers. It consists of two small pieces of plywood between which you sandwich the flowers in layers of absorbent paper (see the illustration opposite). The press is held together by two elastic bands.

Emergency press

In an emergency you can press flowers between the pages of a book or magazine. Turn over the first six pages and insert a layer of tissues, then the flowers, and then another layer of tissues. Gently close the book and place a heavy weight on top.

Layers in a press

Plywood board

Wing nut

Three sheets of
folded recycled paper

Two layers of tissues
or one-way nappy liners

Three sheets of
folded recycled paper

Bolt

Plywood board

TRADITIONAL PRESS

A traditional flower press can be bought from most craft shops or, alternatively, you can make one yourself. It consists of two pieces of heavy-gauge plywood, which form the top and bottom of the press, and these are joined at the corners by four wing nuts and bolts. There is space in the press for up to twenty or thirty layers of absorbent paper and I use the following order for the layers: three sheets of folded recycled paper, one layer of tissues or one-way nappy liners on which you put your flowers, followed by another layer of tissues or one-way nappy liners and three more sheets of folded recycled paper.

Assembled press

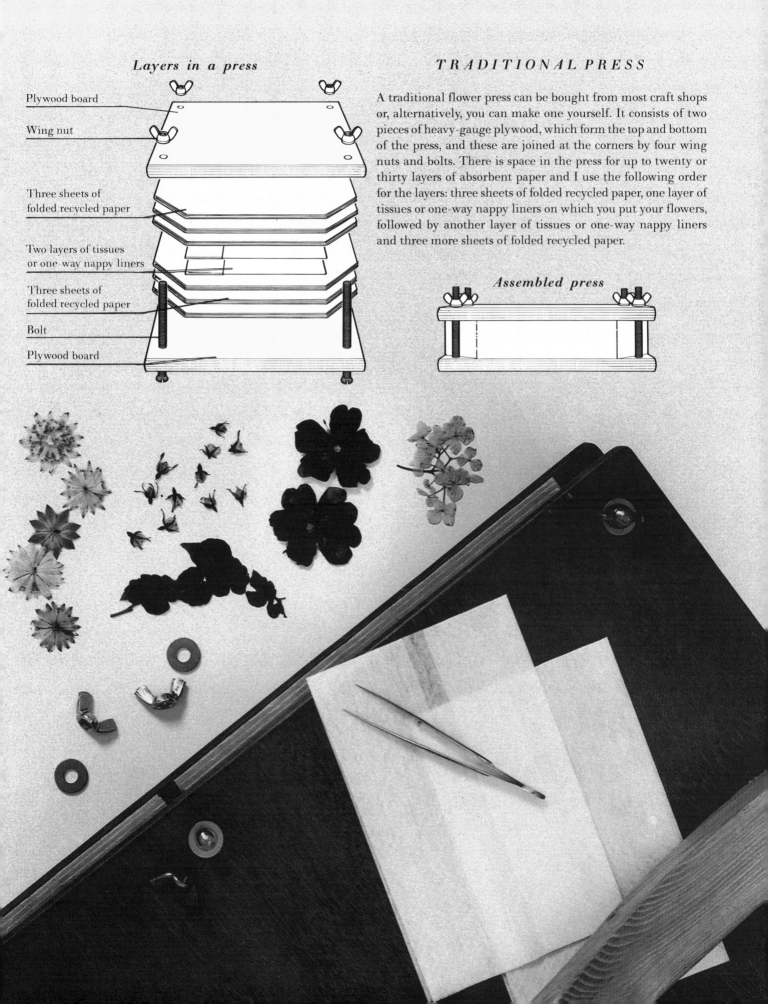

~ *Pressing & Storage* ~

Whatever type of press you use the basic and essential rules of pressing are the same. Speed is of the essence when pressing plant material, and the quicker your material is dried, the brighter the colours will remain.

First you have to build up layers of absorbent paper in the press. I use folded sheets of recycled paper and then a layer of one-way nappy liners, plus extra tissues for juicy plant material, but you can use blotting paper, sugar paper, or newspaper. Lay your flowers and leaves carefully on the nappy liners or tissues, putting as many as possible on to the sheet without them overlapping. Keep material of a similar thickness on the same sheet as this will ensure that the entire sheet receives uniform pressure. Also try to keep *similar* flowers and leaves together as this makes life easier when you are working on your collages.

Cover the material with another layer of nappy liners or tissues and more layers of recycled paper, making sure that the flowers and leaves are not dislodged in the process. These layers should be repeated for each batch of specimens. To apply the correct pressure, tighten the screws on the press until they become stiff.

Unusual Plant Material

When pressing succulent plant material, such as *fruit and vegetables, toadstools* and *fungi*, use very gentle pressure and change the paper and tissues frequently. *Dried flowers*, on the other hand, require very strong pressure.

Quick Drying

I try to dry everything in about two weeks or less (with the exception of fruit and vegetables), by regularly changing the damp recycled paper with dry paper. For the first three or four days, you should change or dry the paper at least once a day. After that you can leave it for two or more days, depending on how dry your material actually is. But remember, *do not* take your specimens out of the

BUILDING THE LAYERS IN A PRESS

1 Fold three sheets of recycled paper in half lengthways and place these in the press. Lay a fourth sheet of recycled paper, folded, on top of these and then open it out again, so that one half of the paper is outside the edge of the press.

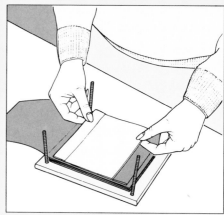

2 Place a layer of one-way nappy liners on top of the recycled paper layers. If you are pressing succulent plant material, such as fruit and vegetables, place an extra layer of tissues in between the recycled paper and the nappy liners.

3 Lay the flowers and leaves carefully on top of the nappy liners, putting as many as possible on to the sheet without them overlapping. Make sure the plant material is of a similar thickness to ensure it receives uniform pressure.

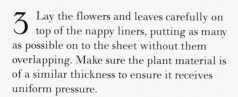
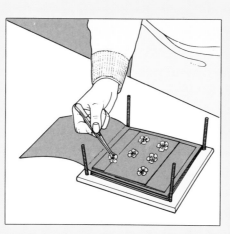

4 Cover the plant material with another layer of nappy liners (and an extra layer of tissues if pressing succulent plant material) and then refold the last sheet of recycled paper over the top. Place a further three sheets on top to complete the layers.

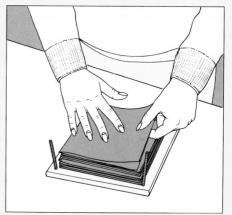

actual nappy liners or tissues on which they have been arranged, as they will be very frail and easily damaged.

Dry the paper in a warm place, such as over a radiator or chair in a warm dry room, or in an airing cupboard. I often return warm paper to the press as this speeds up the drying process. But make sure the paper is not *too* hot or you may end up with "casseroled" flowers! Test the plant material for dryness: if the flowers feel cold and clammy, they are not ready; when they feel crisp and warm, they are dry and ready to use.

Dry Storage

Store the material in a dry place to guard against mould, the arch enemy of pressed flower material. It is advisable to put a sheet of corrugated paper between every dozen or so layers of specimens as this will help the air to circulate. I keep my material in a random fashion, so there is an element of surprise when looking through the sheets, which can result in an inspired collage.

Pressed plant material is prone to attack by small mites that will eventually reduce it to dust. Keep a constant check and at the first sign of these microscopic creatures, give them a quick puff of animal flea powder; this will banish them forever.

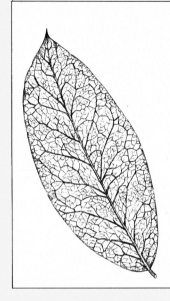

Skeletonized leaves
If you can't find any skeletonized leaves, it is easy to make your own. Collect a supply of leaves in mid-summer (magnolia leaves are the best) and soak them in rainwater for a month to soften the leaf tissue. Then rinse the leaves under running water, and brush them gently with a soft brush to remove the softened tissue. Allow the leaves to dry and then iron them carefully.

STORING PRESSED FLOWERS

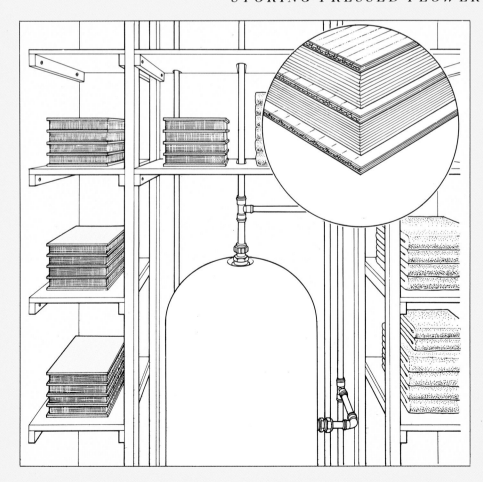

Using your linen cupboard
Store your pressed flowers and other plant material in a dry place with a good circulation of air, to guard against damp and mould. A linen or airing cupboard is ideal, if you have the room. Keep the pressed plant material in the sheet of recycled paper in which it was pressed, but remove the top layer of nappy liners. Stack the sheets one on top of the other, with a sheet of corrugated paper between every dozen of so layers of specimens, to help the air circulate.

~ *Papers & Boards* ~

The paper you use as a backing for your picture will play an important role in the overall impact that your collage will have. I believe that good quality papers, preferably hand-made, are essential. You will be putting time, thought, and part of yourself into your work, so it deserves to be displayed on beautiful paper.

There are many different types of paper and board you can use, of varying weights, textures and colours. A general rule is to use board or heavyweight paper as backing for larger collages, and lighter weight paper for smaller pictures and cards. Some coloured papers are very pretty and can enhance your flower collage; plain white paper will emphasize the colour and form of your compositions, making their effect more dramatic.

You also have a choice of textures. I always use a heavy and textured paper when backing large and heavily embossed collages. The scrunchy plant materials blend beautifully with the grain of the paper. Papers dyed with and containing such materials as bracken and onion skins are also fun to use. Textured machine-made paper is also available and this serves as an excellent substitute for hand-made paper. More formal compositions, with little texture to them, look better displayed on smooth paper.

Unusual Papers

Continental papers such as Italian marbled paper can make interesting backgrounds. Alternatively, you could try some of the beautiful Japanese papers as backings; these can be very thin, so you may need to back them with a cheaper mediumweight white paper. You can also experiment with flock papers and wallpapers, which can give the impression of brocade or rich velvet.

You will also need absorbent papers for pressing your flower material. I use recycled paper but blotting paper, sugar paper or even newspaper can be just as good.

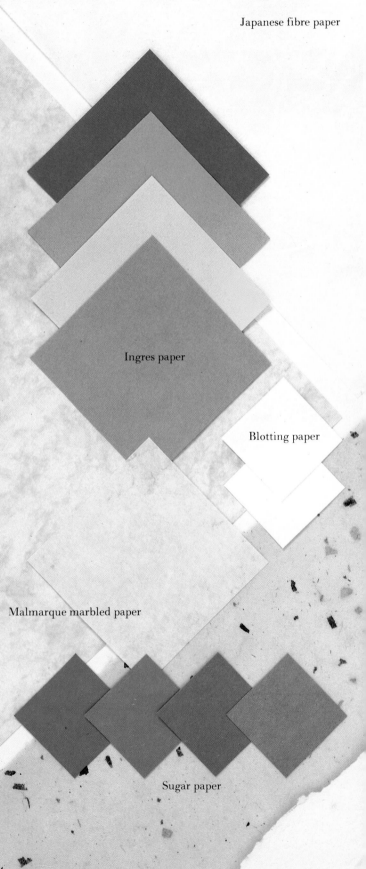

Japanese fibre paper

Ingres paper

Blotting paper

Malmarque marbled paper

Sugar paper

Mounting board

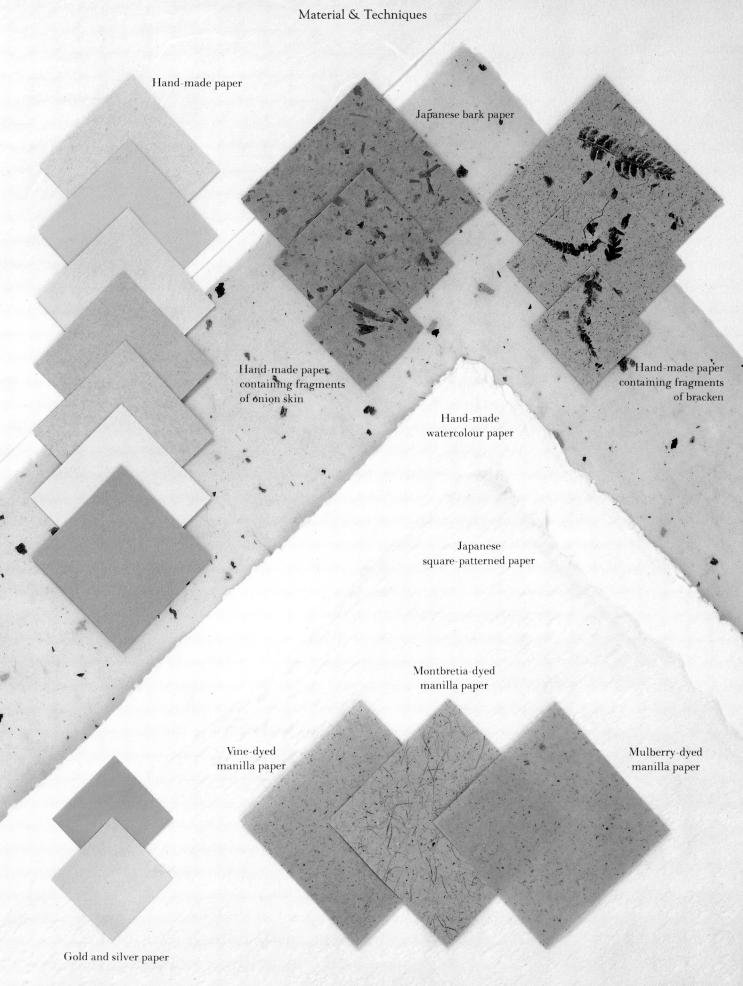

Hand-made paper

Japanese bark paper

Hand-made paper
containing fragments
of onion skin

Hand-made paper
containing fragments
of bracken

Hand-made
watercolour paper

Japanese
square-patterned paper

Montbretia-dyed
manilla paper

Vine-dyed
manilla paper

Mulberry-dyed
manilla paper

Gold and silver paper

~Fabrics~

There is a wide variety of fabric you can use as backings for your pictures, or for making into pillows, sachets or bags. Everyone has a slightly different interpretation as to what is aesthetic. However, there are a few guidelines by which I believe we can all work.

Firstly I recommend that all fabrics used must be natural. Synthetic materials are just not suitable for the pretty, natural image that this work projects. Strong acrylic colours are far too jarring, although it is possible to bleach brightly printed sprigged cottons and chintzes until they are quite pale and look like dimity.

Natural Materials and Dyes

Silks, linens and cottons in neutral shades of coffee, cream, and beige are appropriate for all kinds of pressed flower work. Sew scrim, cotton net or old lace on to unbleached calico for an attractive textured background. Striped cotton ticking, too, can give a modern feel to a brightly coloured flower picture.

You can dye your fabrics with natural dyes, such as lichen, onions, turmeric, marigolds, sloe berries, elderberries and bracken. The results are often quite beautiful, blending subtly with the colours of your pressed flowers. For the detailed techniques of fabric dyeing, see page 108.

Richly coloured silks, brocades and velvets can also be used; they can enrich a flower collage, adding luxury and elegance. Experiment first, to make sure the colours do not overwhelm your flower arrangements.

It is a good idea to back most fabrics with interfacing, as this gives the fabric body and prevents creasing. Alternatively, you can back your fabric with lightweight synthetic wadding for a soft and slightly quilted effect. This can look very pretty for lace pillows and cushions.

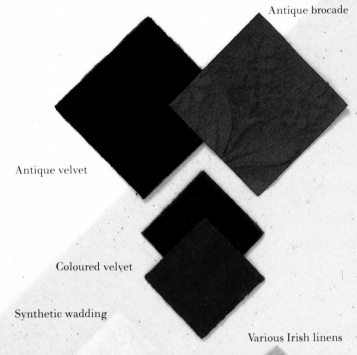

Antique brocade

Antique velvet

Coloured velvet

Synthetic wadding

Various Irish linens

Interfacing

Antique coloured silks

Lichen-dyed silk (left)
and undyed silk

Indian silk

Water-silk taffeta

Scrim

Victorian silk taffeta

Bleached and unbleached cotton prints

Ecclesiastical silks

Calico

Cotton ticking

Lace trimmings

Antique lace

~Making a Picture~

When you first attempt to make a flower picture, allow yourself plenty of time, plenty of space and have everything to hand: glue, card, orange sticks, scissors, plus, of course, lots of pressed plant material. A good idea is to group your pressed flowers according to shape, size or colour, so you don't have to spend a lot of time sifting through a mass of pressed flowers each time you want to glue a specimen on your picture.

It may take you a while to get used to handling forceps or tweezers and you may damage the odd flower or stalk as a result. But don't worry – you will soon gain confidence.

The basic instructions for making a flower picture are outlined below. Once you have mastered the different techniques involved and can handle the plant material with ease, you can begin to experiment and create your own individual flower pictures.

A successful picture is one that is pleasing to look at and does not offend the eye. So it should have a balance both in its composition and in its use of colour. I also think a picture should be *interesting* to look at, so make use of all the varying textures and shapes of plant material that are available in your flower picture.

THE BASIC STEPS

1 Cut out the backing card. Brush rubber-based glue over it. Carefully position the skeletonized leaves on the glued card, starting from centre top.

2 Trim the leaves where they overlap the card. Carefully dip moss and lichen into a saucer of rubber-based glue and then position them on the picture.

3 Hold delicate blossoms with forceps. Dab glue on the back of each flower-centre with an orange stick. Carefully place the flowers in position.

4 Glue sprays of flowers on to the moss. Dab glue on to small leaves with an orange stick and press them gently in position around the edges of the card. Stick small blossoms on the picture.

5 Before completing the picture, turn it on to its reverse side and, holding it gently with one hand, and resting the picture on the table, trim the bottom edge with sharp scissors.

6 Dab glue on to the lower third of long flower stalks with an orange stick. Then, using forceps, tuck the stalks behind flowers and pads of moss. These will complete your flower picture.

The finished picture
With its delicate combination of muted russets and greens, the collage has a mellow, autumnal air.

~ Tricks of the Trade ~

When you first start making your flower collages you will probably feel a little nervous at the prospect of handling fragile blossoms and you are bound to make mistakes and damage the odd flower, or break a stalk or two. Don't worry about this: with practice you will find ways and means of transforming, substituting, altering, improving and mending your work. Damaged material can easily be mended by patching, by hiding the offending portion with something else, or simply by removing and replacing the damaged material. Rubber-based glue is ideal for those who are constantly changing their minds or making mistakes.

Plant material can be joined and altered in a host of ways. If the angle of a stalk or spray offends, then you can carefully break portions off and re-align them when gluing them on to your picture. If you encounter a problem there is almost certainly a way round it, even if you are reduced to cutting up a precious picture and making it into cards! I once ran out of glue when experimenting with a collage but successfully completed it using marmalade!

You can also indulge in a little pressed flower *trompe-l'oeil*. The shapes of leaves can be changed; you can construct your own "designer-made" flowers from odd left-over petals, flower centres, leaves and stalks; or you can make large and complicated flowers out of a graded series of smaller ones placed one on top of the other. Of course as you become more experienced, you will learn to cut corners as well. Pressed flowers is a time-consuming craft and any short cut is worth remembering. Listed below are some of the "tricks of the trade" I have discovered over the years.

Spraying seedheads
Dried seedheads can look very pretty in a flower picture. However, the seeds are liable to fall out, so to fix them in place, spray them with hair lacquer before arranging them in position on your flower picture.

CUTTING CORNERS

- *Spray finished pictures with hair lacquer to stop odd leaves and blossoms falling off.*
- *Iron skeletonized leaves carefully after gathering them — there is no need to press them.*
- *In an emergency, dry plant material in a microwave oven set on defrost. You may need to experiment first so don't use your best specimens.*
- *Swap flower stalks around if, for instance, a longer or a more curved stalk is needed.*
- *Improve a flower by sticking a small umbel or floret in its centre.*
- *Highlight a dark flower by sticking it over a larger paler flower, or by gluing small contrasting florets around the edges of the petals.*
- *Pare clumsy stalks with sharp nail scissors to make them more aesthetic.*
- *Iron out creases in petals and leaves with a cool iron.*
- *Decorate the centres of flowers with small beads or sequins for a glittering, theatrical effect.*
- *If you are short of skeletonized leaves, spray fine veiling with paint and use it as a background.*
- *Add a touch of paint to translucent flowers, such as snowdrops, to enhance their appearance.*
- *Iron mature grass heads, ferns and bracken fronds between two sheets of paper instead of pressing them.*
- *Press and dry fresh leaves by ironing with a cool iron.*
- *Cut plant material into the shape of bows to decorate bouquet pictures.*
- *Use the reverse side of a leaf if it is prettier than the right side.*
- *Use tweezers rather than forceps to handle tiny beads unless you want someone on the other side of the room to catch them!*
- *Reconstruct damaged flowers by gluing the best petals into a flower shape on a small circle of paper.*
- *Trim flowers and foliage if they are too large for your picture.*
- *Spray volatile seedheads with hair lacquer to stop the seeds falling out.*
- *Before pressing strawberries, cut them in half lengthways and remove some of the soft centre. Then pack the back of the fruit with tissues.*
- *Cut out varying shapes of skeletonized leaves by using one leaf as a template, placing it over a larger leaf, and cutting around it.*
- *When the picture is finished, stand it on its end and tap it sharply on a flat surface to remove odd fragments of plant material.*

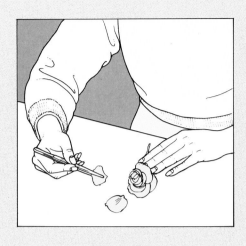
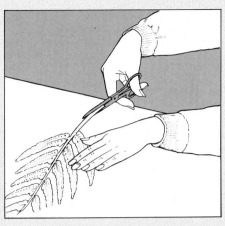

Pens & Inks

As a finishing touch to your flower picture, you may like to add your name and the date, or the title of your picture. Remember to use as fine a pen as possible. I find that a fine technical drawing pen is best for writing on paper and a fine polyacetate-tipped pen for writing on fabric. You could also use a fine-nibbed italic pen or a mapping pen, which you can dip into gold leaf paint or water-soluble ink. Inks are available in a variety of colours; you only need a few basic colours from which you can then mix your own shades.

For drawing surrounds to pictures, use thicker felt-tipped pens, experimenting with the many colours available. Pastel crayons are also very useful; use them to create beautiful backgrounds in soft colours that will blend well with the natural colours of your flowers.

Soft lead pencil

Fine technical drawing pen

Very fine polyacetate-tipped pens

Propelling pencil

Various nibs

Nib reservoir

Italic pen

Fine mapping pen

Pastel crayons

Fine gold marker pen

Gold leaf paint

Water-soluble inks

Water-based felt-tipped pens

Broad silver marker pen

Spirit-based marker pens

Turkey feather quill pen

Drawing inks

Composition, Colour & Texture

*The following pages show you how to
plan your flower pictures: what composition
style to choose, which colours to use,
and how to combine different textures.
You can make a rich, luxuriant
composition in majestic tones of red
and purple, or a soft, romantic picture
using pastel colours and feathery textures.
These pages provide the guide,
but the key is to experiment.*

~Composition~

The composition of your flower pictures is both the overall form of the arrangement as well as the way you combine and group specimens in the arrangement.

Some overall forms are conventional and might inspire you: circular or oval garlands, bouquets and posies, friezes or the repetitive designs of borders. Then there is the form that botanists use to record their specimens with lots of space between them. All of these will bear every interpretation your imagination can come up with. And there is an infinite number of free-form collages to create where the overall composition is random. You might even choose to make compositions that combine forms, a bouquet with a border for example.

Developing a Style

How you combine flowers and other plant material is a matter of your own taste in shape and colour. This is the part of making pressed flower pictures that allows your own style to grow and flourish. You will remember successful combinations and use them again. If you decide on a lush approach, include any material that is aesthetically pleasing to you, mingling sprays, single blossoms, leaves, lichens and mosses. There need be no uniformity — a haphazard arrangement is both natural and charming. With such pictures, I like to create a feeling of depth, using tall spindly specimens in the foreground to partially obscure "distant" blooms.

Garland card
(top right)
An oval garland of roses featuring the exquisite 'Veilchenblau' rose at centre top.

Flower basket
(far right)
This traditional composition is given a modern look against cotton ticking.

Lush frieze *(right)*
This short frieze is a rich profusion of mingled wild and garden flowers, all picked during early summer.

~Simple & Botanical~

My simple and botanical compositions are inspired by the plant drawings found in sixteenth and seventeenth century herbals. The naive simplicity of these drawings is most attractive; single specimen plants, often including the roots, were meticulously drawn in a rather stylized form. Isolated flower-heads and seed capsules were frequently displayed separately alongside the parent plant, and each part was labelled individually.

These pictures originally served a purely instructive purpose but have since come to be regarded as very decorative. It is with this latter purpose in mind that I have developed my botanical style of composition.

Single Specimens

Making a picture from a single pressed flower specimen is one of the easiest to do and a good way to build up your confidence in creating flower pictures. Successful botanical compositions are clear, simple and neat, with lots of white background visible.

You can use any specimen of plant you like; pretty, small plants such as chamomile, threepenny-bit roses and buttercups are good for small cards, but if you are making a larger picture, you could use larger specimens or groups of plants, such as a collection of cottage garden plants, or a group of sweet-smelling herbs.

Taking the picture a stage further, you could make a border of rosebuds or create a pale colour-washed border with no ornamentation at all. For the more elaborate borders, you could make an abstract collage of flowers. Inspiration and ideas can be gleaned from the richly illuminated pages of old herbals.

Botanical Herbal

In my Elizabethan picture, shown opposite, I have displayed a variety of plants that would have been grown in Elizabethan times: old damask roses, ferns, astrantias, scabious, cuckooflowers and lungwort. I gathered most of them from my own garden and then pressed them, the little ferns complete with their roots. Hemlock water-dropwort, cuckooflowers and the old roses are all steeped in herbal lore and have been painted and written about for hundreds of years. Sweetly scented bergamot and the little astrantias are also very old plants. The specimen plants are surrounded by a beautifully coloured border collage, a rich and luxuriant style of composition that contrasts well with the simple specimen plants. The arched rectangle has been edged with little rosebuds in the ornamental fashion of the old herbals.

There are many other themes you can develop and you only need to look to nature for your inspiration.

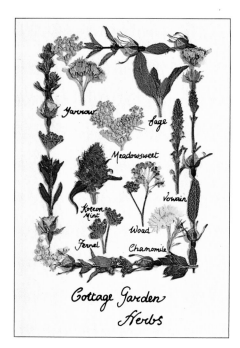

Cottage garden herbs
A collection of cottage garden herbs are displayed simply within a decorative border.

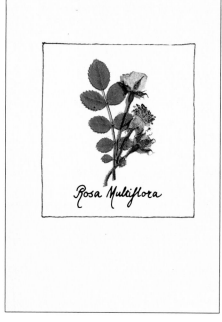

Rosebud card
The sparse arrangement of tiny rosebuds and a rose leaf inside a square border give this card a quiet elegance.

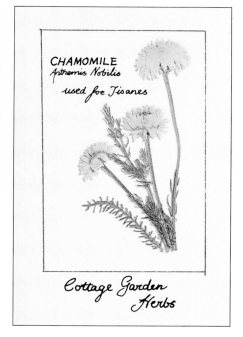

Botanical card
The very starkness of this card adds charm to the lovely specimen of double chamomile.

Elizabethan herbal
*A simple display of old-fashioned Elizabethan-style flowers
is enriched by a colourful, decorative border,
made in a contrasting style of composition.*

~Colour~

The colours you use in your flower picture form an important part of its composition and will determine the overall impact of the design. Bright and vibrant colours, such as reds and yellows, create a strong image and immediately catch one's eye; muted pastel colours convey a feeling of delicacy and softness; while the dark, sombre shades of brown and grey and deep green add a touch of drama and moodiness.

A successful picture will depend upon your appreciation of colour. Some people have an instinctive understanding and feel for colour, but this can also come with experience. For those who are unsure about mixing colours together, a basic knowledge of the theory of colour provides a good starting point.

The Theory of Colour

The colours of the spectrum, from red through to violet, can form a complete circle, each colour progressing to the next. This circle is known as the colour wheel, and is shown here made from a selection of pressed flowers.

The three primary colours — red, yellow and blue — are the strongest colours in the spectrum and you should use these with care, as they can easily dominate and

The colour wheel (right)
All the colours of the spectrum are shown in this colour wheel of pressed flowers. The three primary colours of red, yellow and blue and the three secondary colours of orange, green and violet can be combined in complementary or contrasting colour schemes within your picture.

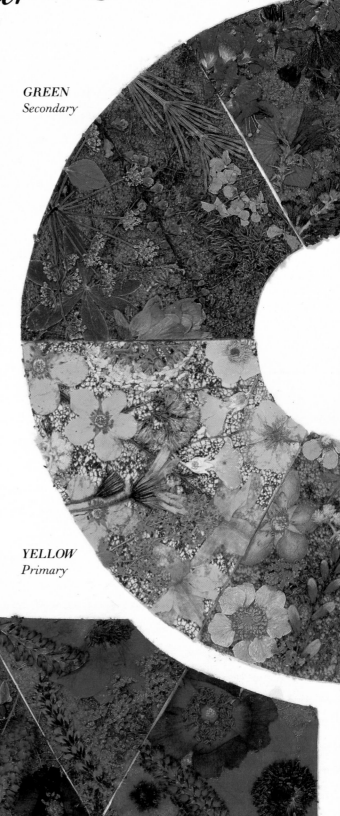

GREEN
Secondary

YELLOW
Primary

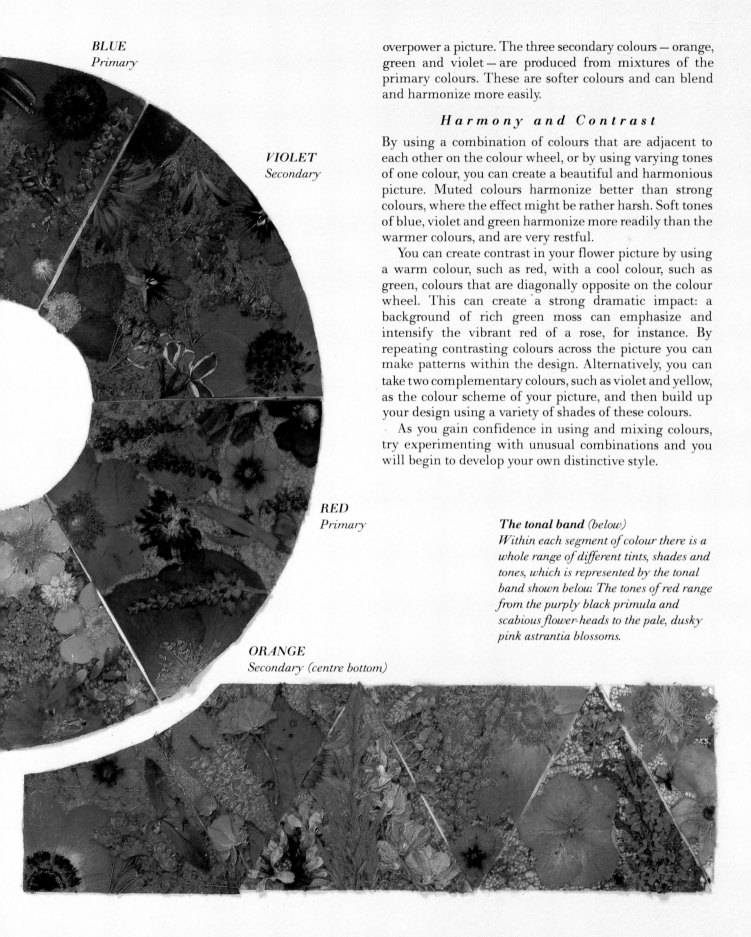

BLUE
Primary

VIOLET
Secondary

RED
Primary

ORANGE
Secondary (centre bottom)

overpower a picture. The three secondary colours — orange, green and violet — are produced from mixtures of the primary colours. These are softer colours and can blend and harmonize more easily.

Harmony and Contrast

By using a combination of colours that are adjacent to each other on the colour wheel, or by using varying tones of one colour, you can create a beautiful and harmonious picture. Muted colours harmonize better than strong colours, where the effect might be rather harsh. Soft tones of blue, violet and green harmonize more readily than the warmer colours, and are very restful.

You can create contrast in your flower picture by using a warm colour, such as red, with a cool colour, such as green, colours that are diagonally opposite on the colour wheel. This can create a strong dramatic impact: a background of rich green moss can emphasize and intensify the vibrant red of a rose, for instance. By repeating contrasting colours across the picture you can make patterns within the design. Alternatively, you can take two complementary colours, such as violet and yellow, as the colour scheme of your picture, and then build up your design using a variety of shades of these colours.

As you gain confidence in using and mixing colours, try experimenting with unusual combinations and you will begin to develop your own distinctive style.

The tonal band *(below)*
Within each segment of colour there is a whole range of different tints, shades and tones, which is represented by the tonal band shown below. The tones of red range from the purply black primula and scabious flower-heads to the pale, dusky pink astrantia blossoms.

~Changing Colour~

Pressed flowers often have a depth of colour and feel of luxury that no fresh flowers can equal, such as the beautiful and velvety crimson old roses. However, it can be fun sometimes to change or enhance these colours to produce a more dramatic and theatrical flower picture.

I had great fun making the picture opposite. All the plant material in it, with the exception of the white everlasting flowers, has been sprayed with different coloured paint — yellow, red, black, green, silver and gold.

The bold red and yellow roses, anemones and hydrangea blooms throw into sharp relief the pure white everlasting flowers with their sunny yellow centres, while a hint of drama is added with the impressive, black spikes of Scots lovage and loosestrife. I sprayed the moss a richer green and the pink cow parsley a deeper pink, while the moss basket was changed to gold.

BEFORE & AFTER COLOURING

Loosestrife

Elder

Scots lovage

Anemone

Sea carrot

Skeletonized leaves

Edwardian basket
With the addition of coloured spray paint, this simple basket of summer blooms has become a lavish, theatrical display.

Texture

Smooth

There is a wealth of smooth plant material you can use in your flower pictures, from velvety rose petals and glossy ivy leaves to tiny, delicate hydrangea blooms. Smooth textured petals and leaves contrast well with the coarser, chunkier plant material shown opposite. Try edging silky rose blooms with clumps of moss and lichen, to give depth and interest to the picture.

The large, soft flower-heads of old roses and anemones can be used to form the focal point of a collage. They will dictate a colour scheme, around which the rest of the collage can be created. Care must be taken in the pressing of smooth plant material, however, as it will be very closely scrutinized. Smaller flowers, such as florets of hydrangea and yarrow add a touch of subtlety to a picture. They can be used to soften the hard edges of larger blooms and to emphasize a dominant feature. Small sprays can also be used as a decorative finishing touch.

Forget-me-not

Potentilla

Virginia creeper

Deutzia

Clematis

Honesty

Cuckooflower

Flowering cherry

Black spleenwort

Primula

Japanese anemone

Ivy

'De Caen' anemone

Hydrangea

Crane's-bill

Yarrow

Old rose

Eryngium

Alder catkins

Monk's-
hood

Meadow
oat-grass

Coarse

Coarse plant material plays a very important role in the composition of my flower pictures, producing a three-dimensional effect, casting shadows and creating depth and interest. But don't overdo the coarse elements in a picture or the result will be too heavy. Instead, mix them with smooth blossoms and leaves for contrast.

There is a wide variety of textured plant material that you can use, in all shapes and sizes and with varying levels of coarseness. There are tall and brittle thistles and grasses, knobbly twigs of pussy willow and witch hazel, heavily laden sprays of catkins and hips, thick springy clumps of moss and marvellously lumpy lichens. Even pressed strawberries, green loganberries, raspberries, blackcurrants and blackberries are all effective, providing an interesting splash of colour as well as unusual texture.

It is useful to keep a ready supply of coarse plant material in fairly neutral colours. Dark brown alder catkins, rich green moss and the pretty pinkish quaking-grass are good examples. This material can then be used to add texture in any composition, without confusing the colour scheme.

Knapweed

Roses

Witch hazel

Rose hips

Hop

Lesser
quaking-
grass

Blackberry

Moss

Ivy berries

Lichen

Bark

Pussy willow

53

Feathery

Feathery plant material has a soothing influence in a flower picture, balancing the effect of the heavy coarse elements and the bright colourful blossoms, and contrasting with sharp and spiky plants.

Delicate sprays of baby's breath and lady's-mantle can be arranged around large, brightly coloured flowers, softening their impact and perhaps correcting a jarring note. The tiny brown flower-heads of great wood-rush can provide a pretty lacy edging around bold shapes, while the pale creamy umbels of sea carrot and cow parsley break up a sharp edge.

The gently tapering leaves of sweet cicely and asparagus fern can shroud and mist bold shapes, subtly altering colours and adding a calming influence. The fluffy beards of traveller's-joy and soft astilbe flower-heads add an intriguing tactile quality to a flower picture.

The colours of feathery sprays and blossoms tend to be pale and neutral, which also adds to their soothing effect. Pale green hemlock water-dropwort and lady's-mantle, creamy yellow sea carrot and elder flowers and the soft white blossoms of baby's breath can be used liberally in most compositions, without affecting the colour scheme.

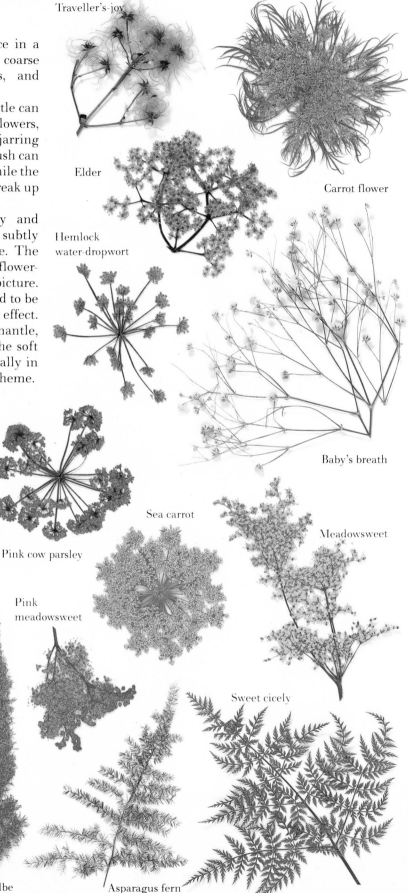

Traveller's-joy

Elder

Carrot flower

Hemlock water-dropwort

Baby's breath

Lady's-mantle

Pink cow parsley

Sea carrot

Meadowsweet

Pink meadowsweet

Allium

Sweet cicely

Great wood-rush

Astilbe

Asparagus fern

54

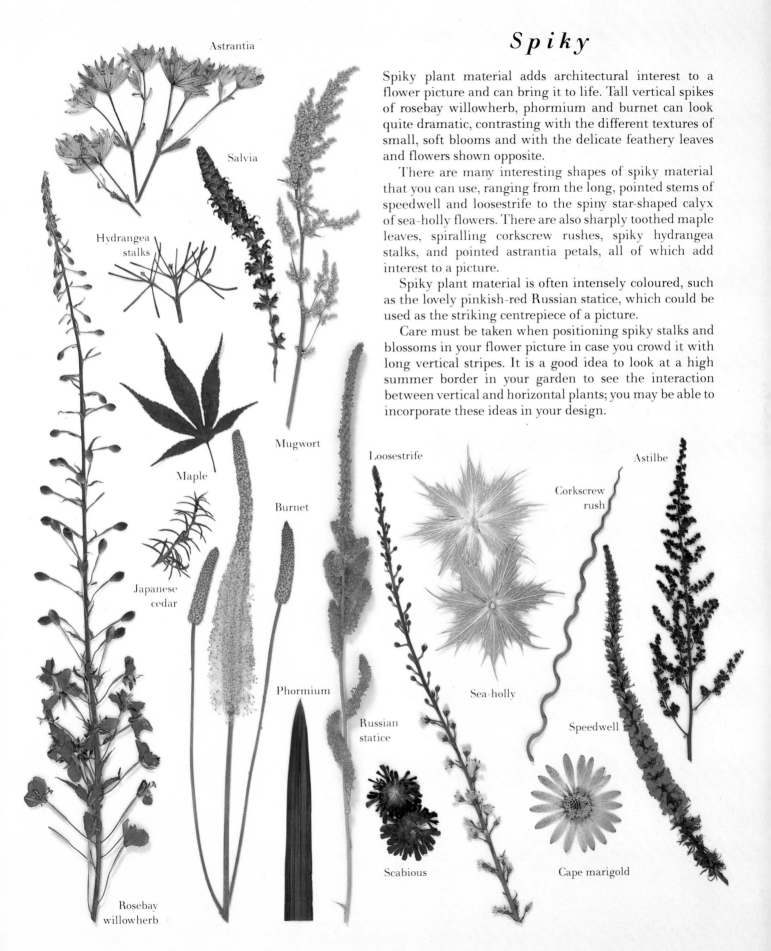

Spiky

Spiky plant material adds architectural interest to a flower picture and can bring it to life. Tall vertical spikes of rosebay willowherb, phormium and burnet can look quite dramatic, contrasting with the different textures of small, soft blooms and with the delicate feathery leaves and flowers shown opposite.

There are many interesting shapes of spiky material that you can use, ranging from the long, pointed stems of speedwell and loosestrife to the spiny star-shaped calyx of sea-holly flowers. There are also sharply toothed maple leaves, spiralling corkscrew rushes, spiky hydrangea stalks, and pointed astrantia petals, all of which add interest to a picture.

Spiky plant material is often intensely coloured, such as the lovely pinkish-red Russian statice, which could be used as the striking centrepiece of a picture.

Care must be taken when positioning spiky stalks and blossoms in your flower picture in case you crowd it with long vertical stripes. It is a good idea to look at a high summer border in your garden to see the interaction between vertical and horizontal plants; you may be able to incorporate these ideas in your design.

Astrantia

Salvia

Hydrangea stalks

Mugwort

Maple

Loosestrife

Astilbe

Corkscrew rush

Burnet

Japanese cedar

Sea-holly

Speedwell

Phormium

Russian statice

Scabious

Cape marigold

Rosebay willowherb

Non-Flower Material

Having magpie tendencies is a great advantage when it comes to collecting non-flower material for my flower pictures. Over the years I have amassed a veritable horde of beads, lace trimmings, ribbons, shells, sea glass, sequins, silk and satin threads, semi-precious stones, buttons, fossils and other intriguing bits and bobs. If you enjoy embroidery and dressmaking, you are bound to have many oddments you can use, otherwise you can experiment with any bric-a-brac you have.

There are lots of imaginative ways of using non-flower material in your flower pictures, all of which add interest,

sparkle and fun. You can glue sequins or beads in flower centres, thread delicate silk ribbons through nosegays and garlands, and you can even make butterflies and moths from silky threads, sequins and beads, to add an element of surprise to a picture. Little shells can nestle amongst mosses and lichens, fossils and unusual pieces of sea glass can be arranged at the base of your picture, and glitter can be sprinkled amongst the foliage. Then there are seeds and spices that you could arrange in haphazard groups, as edgings or even as intriguing garnishes. The possibilities are endless, limited only by your imagination.

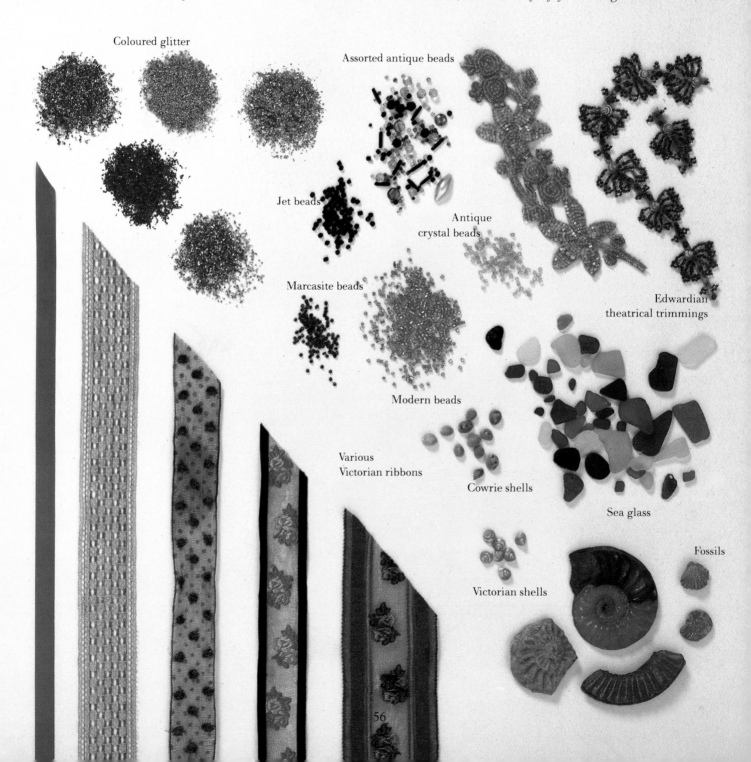

Coloured glitter

Assorted antique beads

Jet beads

Antique
crystal beads

Marcasite beads

Edwardian
theatrical trimmings

Modern beads

Various
Victorian ribbons

Cowrie shells

Sea glass

Fossils

Victorian shells

Flower
Projects

*This section illustrates some different
flower projects you can make with
pressed flowers and other plant material.
Once you gain confidence and become inspired,
try experimenting with your own
designs and interpretations.*

⌐Wild Garden⌐

Pictures such as "wild garden" opposite are closest to my heart. Born of a life-long obsession with flowers and gardening, they reflect my delightful garden. They are my flower borders, only better, because every plant is exactly where I want it to be with no bare soil and every nook and cranny occupied. The effect is rich and luxuriant but slightly mysterious, the composition suggesting hidden treasures.

These collages are therapeutic both to make and to examine. Your inspiration need not be restricted to the garden; remove the curtain of skeletonized leaves and colour-wash a blue sky and you can create a meadow picture. Hedgerow pictures are possible, even pictures inspired by fens and moors. Here, the backdrop of skeletonized leaves adds shadow, the mosses and lichens richness and texture, and the many and varied flowers, fascination. Keep the lower half of the picture dark and rich, then gradually introduce a variety of flowers, buds and leaves and allow them to fade away into an undulating horizon of spikes and blossoms.

ELEMENTS OF THE WILD GARDEN

Astrantia

Sea-holly

Fuchsia

Eryngium

Corkscrew rush

Blackberry

Pink cow parsley

Astilbe

Old rose

OTHER ELEMENTS

Baby's breath	Moss
Deutzia	Potentilla
Hydrangea	Sea carrot
Lichen	Skeletonized leaves

HOW TO MAKE A WILD GARDEN

1 Cut out a backing sheet to the required size and brush a thin layer of glue over it. Stick a patchwork of skeletonized leaves on to the backing, starting at the top and working gradually down towards the base.

2 Dip moss and lichens lightly in glue and then press them into place. Hold each flower spray with forceps and dab glue on the lower third of the stalk with an orange stick. Press the sprays in place.

3 Gradually fill in the collage. Hold each flower-head with forceps and dab a little glue in the centre. Stick them on the picture, small flowers in groups and larger blooms in an undulating horizon. Decorate the moss with small flower sprays.

4 Stick tiny flowers around the larger blooms. Add long spiky sprays by gluing and tucking the ends into the moss. Fill in any gaps between flowers with moss. Trim the bottom edge of the picture with scissors and glue it on to a mount.

The wild garden
*The rich green moss intensifies the deep reds and yellows
of the surrounding flowers, creating depth and mood.*

59

~Flower Baskets~

What about creating a moss-lined "basket" using bracken fronds and making it overflow with pressed flowers, mosses, lichens and skeletonized leaves? You can mingle and use plant material gathered during all four seasons, including thin flower spikes of plantain and dock, panicles of wild clematis and ragwort, marigolds, buttercups, astrantias and avens, in fact any plant material from the cornucopia available to us.

Inspirational Ideas

The picture opposite has a strong orange bias, but most combinations will look lovely and give a feeling of rural abundance. A bowl of June flowers, a rich canvas of blossoms and fruits, a collection of blooms from your own garden—all these could be inspirational when filling your basket. Try mixing the unlikely—an unfurling fern frond and a new green seedhead for example, or oats with wild clematis. Avoid adding material that looks clumsy, however. If a stalk is too thick, then pare it to a sliver, and if necessary fillet fern fronds so that the eye is drawn to the intriguing ammonite curl and not to a thick, fuzzy stalk! It is best to begin with an outline of bold, spiky plants and then fill the gaps with smaller flowers.

You can spray the bracken basket a different colour and embellish it with lichens, overflowing blossoms, or even a snail shell. Quaint old wicker baskets are a good source of inspiration. Stand well back from your picture and assess the balance, remembering that the material used should appear to sit in the basket comfortably. If there is a jarring note then stick something over it—rich green moss can work miracles when all else fails.

ELEMENTS OF THE FLOWER BASKET

Astrantia

Meadow oat-grass

Potentilla

Ragwort

Clematis

Montbretia

Young fern frond

Hydrangea

OTHER ELEMENTS

Bracken	Goldenrod	Primula
Burnet	Lady's-mantle	Sea-holly
Everlasting	Lichen	Skeletonized leaves
Ferns	Moss	Wild carrot

HOW TO MAKE A FLOWER BASKET

1 Cut out a basket shape from a piece of card. Dip moss lightly in a saucer of glue and then stick it on the basket shape. Pack the clumps of moss tightly, making sure that no card is visible.

2 Trim several bracken fronds to the size of the basket. Dab glue along each frond with an orange stick, then, using forceps, stick the fronds on the moss. Select the flowers to be displayed.

3 Glue the basket on to a mount. Arrange bold and spiky plant material in a skeleton outline above the basket and glue in place. Fill in with groups of blossoms, long-stemmed fern fronds, moss and lichens.

High summer basket
Both the colour scheme of bold oranges, with yellows, browns and greens, and the overflowing composition of this picture suggest the abundance of midsummer.

~ Greetings Cards ~

Greetings cards are easy and rewarding to make and there are many decorative styles that you can use.

A "Get Well" card, decorated with a posy of pretty and varied flowers, will constantly draw the eyes of someone confined to bed. A garland of blossoms surrounding an inscription could be made into a birthday or anniversary card. Festive Christmas cards provide the ideal opportunity to experiment with gold and silver paint and glitter, as well as with seasonal plants and berries. Time and thought should be spent creating a truly romantic Valentine card; choose the prettiest lace and the loveliest silk, and take time to select your most beautiful flowers. A hand-made card can often mean far more to the recipient than one that has been bought.

Bookmarks and Gift Tags

These can be decorated in a similar way to the greetings cards, using a variety of styles, but on a smaller scale. Little gift labels decorated with the tips of flower spikes, newly formed leaves, tiny florets and small unopened buds can all look enchanting.

The arrangement of the flowers on bookmarks should be slightly elongated to keep a sense of balance on the long narrow piece of card. To complete the bookmark or gift tag, punch a hole at the bottom of the card, and then loop through a length of ribbon.

MAKING A CARD

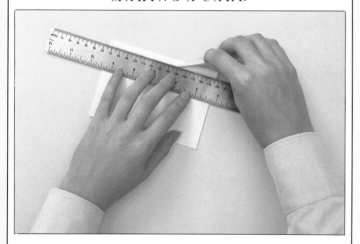

Cut out a rectangle of hand-made paper to measure approximately 18 cm long by 12 cm wide (8 x 4 in). Fold the paper in half lengthways. Place a ruler about 2 mm (⅛ in) from the edge of the fold as shown above and hold it firmly in place with one hand. Holding a bone folder (or an appropriate substitute) in your other hand, run it over the paper along the edge of the ruler, to flatten and sharpen the fold. You can now decorate the front of your card with pressed flowers and leaves.

Bookmarks and gift tags (above)
These decorative bookmarks and gift tags were very easy to make. The simplest design consists of a single specimen flower framed in a narrow border, while the more abstract design is a "random" collage of flowers and leaves, cut into rectangular shapes, and then glued on the bookmark or tag.

Random flower collage (below)
A colourful, abstract design of blossoms, leaves and mosses.

Festive Christmas wreath (above)
This tiny wreath was made with ivy leaves, berries and fir leaves and decorated with a bright red ribbon.

Romantic Valentine card (above)
A heart made from threepenny-bit rosebuds and frilled lace is framed by a pretty lace border.

Garland card (above)
A simple yet effective design of tiny forget-me-nots, violets, ivy leaves and avens.

A seashore theme (above)
A pleasing arrangement of seaside plants, shells and seaweeds make for an unusual greetings card.

Favourite summer flowers (above)
A bouquet arrangement of small summer flowers is displayed simply against a contrasting background.

⌒ *Pot Pourri* ⌒

Although homes were already being perfumed by mixes of scented flowers, herbs, and spices by the sixteenth century, it was not until the mid-eighteenth century that the term "pot pourri" came into common usage. Originally "pot pourri" was a culinary term meaning a stock-pot of mixed vegetables and meat (its direct translation is "rotten pot"), but the phrase came to mean a mixture of scented plant materials that were used to perfume the home. Rose petals were the most important ingredients, hence the term "rose bowl", and were almost always used in the early recipes. Scented orange flowers were often mixed with rose petals, and spices and fixatives were also included, the latter often of animal derivation, such as musk, civet, ambergris, and castor.

The traditional pot pourri contained the following five groups of ingredients: scented flowers and petals, or woods, roots and barks; herbs; spices; fixatives; and essential oils. Today, pot pourri has the same constituents, although we tend to use vegetable rather than animal fixatives. There is really no mystique surrounding the making of pot pourri and the proportions of ingredients in every recipe can be varied enormously, depending upon what is to hand. You will always require most material from the first group, which will set the theme of the mix. These days we include many unperfumed flowers to improve the appearance of a mix; in the same way we also incorporate brightly coloured, or intriguingly shaped, berries, slices of dried exotic fruits, and seed-heads. We rely much more than our ancestors on essential oils to impart the fragrance of our choice to each mixture.

There is a tendency nowadays to introduce non-floral scents into our homes, such as fruity and oriental perfumes or the more mellow notes of balsam and wood, but the fragramce of a pot pourri depends entirely upon personal taste. A pot pourri today can be richly traditional, cottagey, woody, musky, fruity, or it can even emit a deep, masculine perfume. Visually it can consist of shades of one colour, look highly decorative, or be just a lovely chintzy mixture. The perfume of the garden can be immortalized in the faded, papery beauty of the dried flowers and leaves of a pot pourri. The petals may have lost their moist bloom and heady fresh fragrance, but there remains an exquisite charm and shadowy perfume in the delicate dried blossoms.

Drying & Blending

*F*lat blooms and individual leaves and petals lend themselves to drying flat, as to umbelliferous flowers, lichens, mosses, and berries. Many herbs and sprays of smaller flowers are traditionally dried by hanging them in bunches. Roses, too, can be dried by this method, but the loveliest open blooms should be dried flat and used to decorate the top of a mix. Pot pourri can be made using either the dry or the moist method. Dry pot pourris are easy to make, and look pretty, lending themselves to decorative presentation. Moist pot pourris take longer to make, and are visually less attractive, but they are well worth the effort for their rich, long-lasting fragrances.

Hang-drying

Hang-drying in bunches is the best way to dry herbs, such as lavender; flower sprays, such as lady's mantle; single flowers with larger heads, such as pinks; and large leaves, such as angelica.

Gather the herbs for drying just before they flower, unless of course you wish to dry the flowers as well. Pick flowers in bud or newly opened: a full-blown flower will never dry well. Make sure that the plant material is absolutely dry when you harvest it: noon on a fine day is ideal.

Any dry, airy place is suitable for hang-drying bunches of plant material: in a warm kitchen; over a radiator; in an airing cupboard; or even in an attic. String bunches of herbs and flowers where they can be seen for a continually changing decoration that allows you to observe the intriguing drying process. Attach a line or two across a room or cupboard and hang the bunches from them: you will be surprised at the number of bunches you can fit on a line only 60cm (2ft) long. Tie each bunch together and to the line with a band of nylon cut from a pair of tights: as each bunch dries and the stalks shrink, the nylon contracts, keeping the bunch tightly packed.

It is a good idea to remove most of the leaves from the flower stalks to allow the air to circulate freely around the stems and flower heads. This reduces the risk of mildew appearing before the plant material dries, and speeds up the

drying process. If hang-drying roses, remove the thorns from the stalks for ease of handling. Bunch together no more than six sprays of herbs or flowers, to enable the material to dry out quickly and minimize the risk of mildew. Take great care when hang-drying flowers, particularly those with larger heads, which are easily crumpled during the drying process. Cut the stalks to different lengths so that, when bunched, the flower heads are staggered and do not touch one another. If sprays and umbels are too crowded, remove a flower head or two, but remember that the material shrinks as it dries, gradually requiring less room.

Herbs and flowers vary in the length of time that they take to become crisply dry, depending on how dry and airy the situation, and how thick the leaves and flowers. Do not hang them in strong sunlight, as, in most cases, the flower colours will fade, and remember that the faster the material dries, the more colour it retains.

If you wish to store herbs and flowers after drying them, strip the sprays and stalks of leaves and flowers, and store them in a dry place. Keep them in boxes or large bags and label each of them for future reference.

DRYING A BUNCH OF FLOWERS

1 Choose a fine, dry day to pick the flowers. Select blooms that are in bud or newly opened, and do not pick too many, for they will wilt before you can deal with them. Sort through the fresh flowers carefully and discard any damaged ones.

2 Remove leaves from the flower stalks to allow air to circulate around them. If the leaves are aromatic or pretty, leave a few on the stems and remove and use them after the flowers have dried. Trim the stems to varying lengths.

3 Bunch together about six stems, making sure that the flower heads are not touching one another. Check that none of the petals is twisted or crushed. It is important to keep the heads separate, so that they dry quickly and remain intact.

4 *Tie the bunch together with a band of elasticated nylon cut from a pair of tights. Loop the nylon around the stems and pull tight. Hang the bunch from a line strung across the drying area. Make sure that the flowers are not touching anything.*

Subdued decoration
Making an attractive display in themselves, the bunches of cottage herbs and flowers hang-drying here are (from left to right): variegated balm, lady's mantle, wormwood, and the enormous leaves of elecampane.

DRYING A BUNCH OF ROSES

Colourful display
Stagger the flower heads along the line
to keep them well separated, otherwise
they will dry crumpled and twisted.
The bunches drying here are (from left to
right): marsh-mallow, larkspur, cornflowers,
and modern and old-fashioned roses.

*1 When drying roses by the hanging
method, it is best to remove all the
thorns from the stems to make them easier
and safer to handle. Cut them off with a
sharp pair of scissors or snap them off.*

*2 To allow the air to circulate freely
around the stalks and speed up the
drying time, remove the leaves. Stagger the
blooms in the bunch (see p.66) and hang
them to dry. (To dry leaves, see p.69.)*

Drying flat

*If the material for drying is delicate or thick, if you need to use
only flower petals, or if you require decorative flower heads, then
it is best to dry the material flat.*

Fragile or dense flowers and leaves that are important scented ingredients in pot pourri are best dried flat. They include fragrant jonquils, daffodils, irises, violets, lilies, honeysuckle, wallflowers, and some scented leaves, such as myrtle, eucalyptus, scented-geranium, and sweet briar.

In addition, I take great care to dry some flowers flat that are not necessarily perfumed, but whose shape and form are highly decorative. Nearly all the single flower heads that are to be used decoratively, such as potentillas, anemones, and roses, are better dried separately on a flat surface. Some decorative double flowers are also best dried flat. They include: double primroses, marsh marigolds, ranunculus, geums, feverfew, and double roses. Arrange such flowers carefully so that they dry in as natural a shape as possible. Another important group of flowers that I like to dry flat are the delicate umbelliferous blooms, which add a gossamer touch to a pot pourri. They include the beautiful heads of wild carrot, sweet cicely, cow parsley, and fennel flowers.

Rose petals, the most important ingredient in the majority of pot pourris, can be dried only by the flat method. Gather them when they are quite dry – midday on a fine day is best – and choose petals from newly opened roses when their perfume is at its strongest. Dry the petals in layers no more than two petals deep and shuffle them daily. If the petals are to be used in a dry pot pourri (see p.72), leave them until they are crisply dry, usually about a week later. If the petals are to be used in a moist pot pourri (see p.87), they will be ready in a couple of days when placed in a warm, airy spot; they will then be partially dry and quite leathery.

Certain leaves, by virtue of their shape or colour, should be carefully dried

flat for decorative purposes. They include the intriguingly fluted leaves of curled wood sage and forest-green *Rosa rugosa* leaves. Obviously, berries, fruits, and all citrus peels must be dried flat rather than by hanging.

To dry material flat, lay the petals, leaves, or fruit in a warm room on tea trays, sheets of recycled paper or newspaper, lengths of muslin stretched across two pieces of wood, or even purpose-built racks of narrow and closely slotted wood. Most flowers and leaves dry best when positioned face-up. Take care when laying them out: decorative blooms, such as double flower heads, should not, on any account, touch one another; and single petals will not dry out well if stacked more than two layers deep. The length of time needed for the material to dry ranges from a couple of days to a week or more, depending upon the drying conditions and the plant material. When ready, it should feel crisp and warm to the touch, and the colours should remain bright, particularly if the plant material has been kept out of strong sunlight. In fact, most dark-red roses will retain their colour even if dried in the sun. The material will, of course, shrink considerably during the drying process. If you do not wish to use the material straight away, store it in individually marked boxes in a warm, dry place, such as an airing cupboard.

The many-splendoured rose
Most parts of the rose plant can be used in a pot pourri. If it is to be highly perfumed, the petals will play the most important role. Whole blooms of the perfumed rose will enrich a mix visually, as will opening buds, and even small, tight, green ones. Many rose leaves dry to a luxuriant green, and some are slightly perfumed, as are a number of rose roots.

Rose blooms for decoration

Rose leaves

Rose petals

69

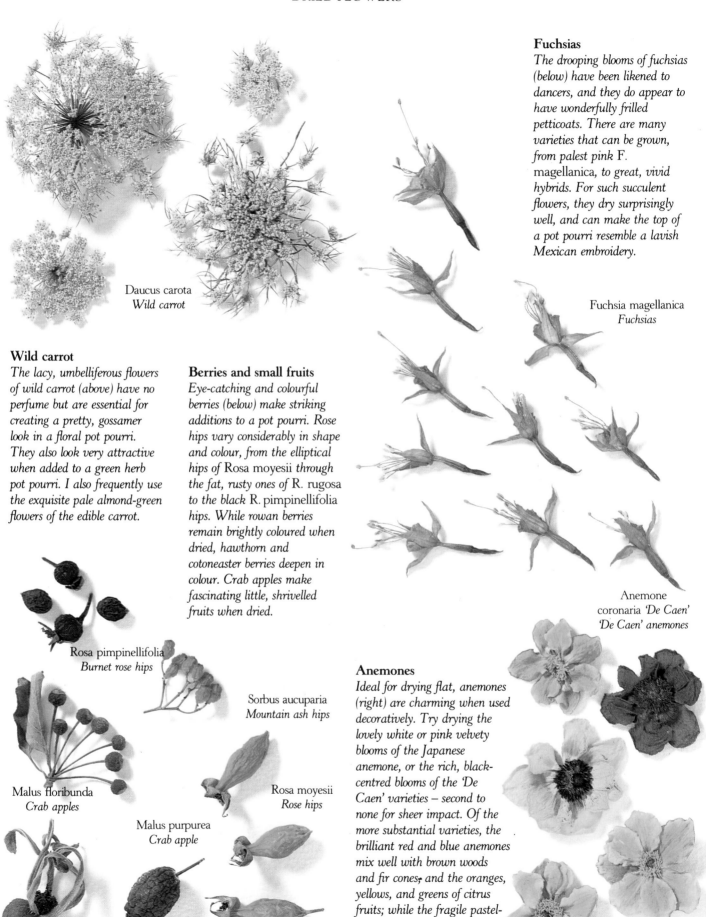

Fuchsias
The drooping blooms of fuchsias (below) have been likened to dancers, and they do appear to have wonderfully frilled petticoats. There are many varieties that can be grown, from palest pink F. magellanica, to great, vivid hybrids. For such succulent flowers, they dry surprisingly well, and can make the top of a pot pourri resemble a lavish Mexican embroidery.

Daucus carota
Wild carrot

Fuchsia magellanica
Fuchsias

Wild carrot
The lacy, umbelliferous flowers of wild carrot (above) have no perfume but are essential for creating a pretty, gossamer look in a floral pot pourri. They also look very attractive when added to a green herb pot pourri. I also frequently use the exquisite pale almond-green flowers of the edible carrot.

Berries and small fruits
Eye-catching and colourful berries (below) make striking additions to a pot pourri. Rose hips vary considerably in shape and colour, from the elliptical hips of Rosa moyesii *through the fat, rusty ones of* R. rugosa *to the black* R. pimpinellifolia *hips. While rowan berries remain brightly coloured when dried, hawthorn and cotoneaster berries deepen in colour. Crab apples make fascinating little, shrivelled fruits when dried.*

Anemone
coronaria 'De Caen'
'De Caen' anemones

Rosa pimpinellifolia
Burnet rose hips

Sorbus aucuparia
Mountain ash hips

Anemones
Ideal for drying flat, anemones (right) are charming when used decoratively. Try drying the lovely white or pink velvety blooms of the Japanese anemone, or the rich, black-centred blooms of the 'De Caen' varieties – second to none for sheer impact. Of the more substantial varieties, the brilliant red and blue anemones mix well with brown woods and fir cones, and the oranges, yellows, and greens of citrus fruits; while the fragile pastel-coloured ones are better suited to cottage mixes.

Malus floribunda
Crab apples

Rosa moyesii
Rose hips

Malus purpurea
Crab apple

Rosa rugosa
Rose hip

Anemone x hybrida
Anemones

Teucrium scorodonia
'Crispum Marginatum'
Curled wood sage

Bergamot

Grown in our gardens for centuries, the old purple bergamot (right) is still a favourite. All varieties of bergamot have delicious, orange-scented leaves. The flowers are also fragrant, and their unusual shape makes them perfect for decorating the surface of a pot pourri.

Monarda didyma
Bergamot

Curled wood sage

The deep pine-green leaves of curled wood sage (above) retain their colour well, and their elaborately ruffled edges are sensational. They are ideal for making decorative borders in an open pot pourri. The plant's near relative – the wild wood sage – has dark, velvety leaves, which are also worth drying.

Potentilla *spp.*
Shrubby and herbaceous
Potentillas

Potentillas

Potentillas (left) are easy to grow, and add an enormous variety of colour to a pot pourri. Scatter the yellow and orange blooms in the nooks and crannies of a bulky citrus pot pourri; garnish an Elizabethan pot pourri with the rich red ones; and use the black-centred, strawberry-pink flowers to enliven any kind of pot pourri.

Tree mallow

Tree mallow flowers (below), which are pink when fresh, dry to resemble scraps of blue tissue paper. Flowers from this family are exciting to dry, as one is never certain exactly what shade of blue they will turn out to be. With any luck, it will be a very intense parma-violet, which is bound to dominate a pot pourri.

Lavatera arborea
Tree mallow

Hydrangeas

The lovely misty colours of blue, pink, and cream hydrangea flowers (right), and the sheer volume of their blooms, make them indispensable to pot pourri. Perhaps the loveliest of all pot pourris is one in which hydrangeas of all the sugared-almond colours are mixed with herbs and some dark green leaves. You can even spray hydrangea flowers gold or silver to decorate such a pot pourri, which is the prettiest of mixes.

Hydrangea *spp.*
Hydrangeas

Making pot pourri

There are two basic methods of making pot pourri: the dry method and the moist method. Dry pot pourris are more attractive to look at but moist pot pourris are more highly scented.

There are five basic groups of ingredients in a dry pot pourri: scented flowers, herbs, spices, fixatives, and essential oils. The first and most important group is that of the scented and decorative materials, which may be flowers, wood, bark, or fruit (see pp,74–86). These will set the theme of your pot pourri. Secondly come the scented herbs (see p.76), of which lavender is the most important and most frequently used. Rosemary, mints, balms, bergamot and thymes are also commonly used. Their perfumes add interest to the dominant perfume of a mix, providing it with more complexity.

The next group is the spices (see p.80) with their warm, sweet smell; they add richness, depth, and sometimes a piquant note to the general bouquet. The fourth group is composed of fixatives (see p.84), without which the perfume of the pot pourri would very quickly be lost. They fix, or hold, and absorb the scents of all the other ingredients, often contributing their own fragrance as well. There are fixatives in all groups of vegetative materials, but you can rely on the easily obtainable orris root powder and gum benzoin, unless, of course, you have other, more obscure fixatives to hand in the kitchen.

The last group comprises the essential oils (see p.86), which can either dictate the perfume of a pot pourri entirely, or simply contribute to it, depending on how much scented plant material you have included. Dried citrus peel can also be added to a pot pourri.

The two methods

A dry pot pourri is by far the easiest to make and the most popular, for the pot pourri is finished as soon as the dried materials have been mixed, although the mix should be allowed to mature for a few weeks before being displayed in a room or used to fill pillows or sachets.

Moist pot pourri is more time-consuming to create. It is made in two stages: creating a moist "stock-pot" of highly scented petals, which involves a curing process, and then combining this mixture with all the other dry ingredients. The cured stock-pot replaces the first group of ingredients in a dry pot pourri. The perfume of a moist pot pourri is delicious. Not only is it stronger than that of a dry mix, but it is alluringly rich, too. Moist pot pourris are not pretty to look at, so they are best contained in a jar or box with a perforated lid to allow the scent to escape.

MAKING A DRY POT POURRI

1 In a small bowl, place the ground spices (2 teaspoons cinnamon powder and ½ teaspoon grated nutmeg) and the fixative (25g/1oz orris root powder). Add six drops of essential oil. If you want a very strongly scented mix, add a little more oil.

2 Thoroughly mix the oil, fixative and spices. Rub the mixture between your first two fingers and thumb as though you were rubbing fat into flour. This will ensure that all the scent of the essential oil is fixed and provide a strong bouquet.

3 In a separate mixing bowl, place the remaining dry ingredients (1 litre/ 1 quart fragrant petals, 50g/2oz mixed sweet herbs, 25g/1oz lavender, ½ teaspoon whole cloves, and ¼ vanilla pod). In a dry place, store the decorative dried flower heads.

Essential oil

Mixing bowl

Small bowl

Spices and fixative

Airtight container

Flower petals

Mixed sweet herbs, including lavender

4 Pour the mixture of fixative, spices and oil into the mixing bowl that contains the bulk of the dry ingredients. Mix together thoroughly to ensure that the oil, fixative, and spices are evenly distributed throughout the pot pourri.

5 Place the mixture in an airtight container and leave in a dark place for at least six weeks. Shake the container every day for the first week. The longer you leave the pot pourri, the more mature the fragrance will become.

6 After a minimum of six weeks, transfer the pot pourri to a decorative open bowl. Decorate the top with the dried flower heads that you set aside. Reseal in the storage container any of the mix you do not yet wish to use.

Roses

Rose blooms and petals are the most important ingredients in many pot pourris. They add a beautiful perfume and a wonderful depth of colour. Of the rich, dark, old-fashioned roses, the damask and centifolia varieties emit the strongest scents, although all the old roses are fragrant and perfectly suited to pot pourri. Many of the colourful modern hybrid tea roses also have a sweet fresh perfume, and their elegant, half-open buds accentuate the charm of a mix. Just as lovely are the large petals of many of the hybrid teas. The dark-red ones are my favourites, as their colour and velvety texture lends rich substance to a pot pourri.

Old-fashioned and shrub roses
These sumptuous roses contain distinctive perfumes, from the heavy scents of the damask and centifolia roses to the peppery fragrance of 'Cecily Brunner'.

Modern roses
*The sophisticated beauty of
these roses is entirely different
from the unruly charm of the
old-fashioned and shrub roses.
From magenta to blush-pink
and from apricot to primrose-
yellow, the range of colour of
the hybrid teas is enormous
and they dry very well.*

75

Subtly scented herbs

The lovely flowers of this selection of gently perfumed herbs range from soft sprays of meadowsweet to imposing yellow heads of achillea, and the leaves vary greatly in shape, texture, and colour. All are easy to obtain and grow, and every one can make a valuable contribution to a pot pourri. Even flowers from the humble mint look delightful when dried, and the leaves of this herb are especially useful when creating a fresh, piquant pot pourri, adding both strength of colour and scent.

Thymus *x* citriodorus
Lemon thyme

Salvia pratensis tenorii
Meadow sage

Mentha *x* spicata
Spearmint

Apium
graveolens
Wild celery

Mentha *x* piperita
Peppermint

Rosmarinus officinalis *'Aureus'*
Variegated rosemary

Artemisia dracunculus
French tarragon

Salvia officinalis *'Purpurascens'*
Purple sage

Ocimum basilicum
'Purpurascens'
Dark opal basil

Achillea millefolium
Wild yarrow

Achillea filipendulina
Yarrow

Achillea millefolium
'Cerise Queen'
Yarrow

Inula magnifica
Elecampane

Melissa officinalis *'Aurea'*
Lemon-scented variegated balm

Filipendula palmata
Meadowsweet

Filipendula ulmaria
Meadowsweet

Filipendula rubra
Queen of the Prairie

Strongly scented herbs

Many of the herbs shown on these pages come from the Mediterranean region, and prefer a warm, dry situation in the garden. Soft to the touch, their lovely foliage (and occasionally their flowers) is usually aromatic. Lavender, with its distinctive fragrance, is a traditional and often essential ingredient in a pot pourri, and can be included in almost any mix. The silver leaves and the often pale-coloured flowers add refinement.

Salvia officinalis 'Tricolor'
Variegated sage

Lavandula angustifolia
Lavender

white

mauve

Salvia sclarea
Clary sage

pink

Lavandula stoechas
Lavender

Origanum dictamnus
Cretan dittany

Pelargonium
crispum
'Variegatum'
*Scented white
variegated
geranium*

Artemisia ludoviciana *'Silver Queen'*
White sage

Althaea officinalis
Marsh-mallow

Perovskia atriplicifolia
Perovskia

Mentha longifolia
Horsemint

Verbena hastata
Vervain

Artemisia pedemontana
Artemisia

Spices, seeds, woods, conifers, and roots

Warm, sweet-smelling spices, aromatic woods, and softly scented roots are all important to pot pourri, lending a depth and piquancy to the fragrance of a mix. Most recipes call for some spices, which range in aroma from subtle and shadowy to strong and dominant, and a few call for scented woods, such as conifer needles, buds, and tips. Sweet flag, geranium, sweet cicely, angelica, and elecampane all have aromatic roots as well as scented leaves. Decorative seed heads, such as fluffy clematis, pussy willow catkins, and tiny alder cones, all make a pot pourri more interesting to look at, as do the delightful little scaled lockets of hop, which can also be used in sleep pillows.

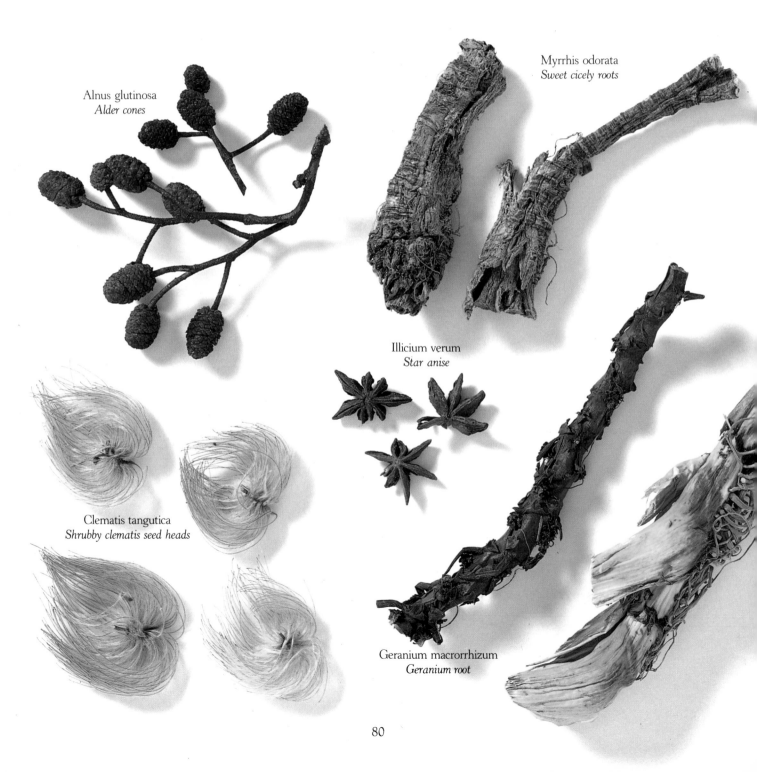

Alnus glutinosa
Alder cones

Myrrhis odorata
Sweet cicely roots

Illicium verum
Star anise

Clematis tangutica
Shrubby clematis seed heads

Geranium macrorrhizum
Geranium root

Geum urbanum
Herb bennet

Angelica archangelica
Angelica root

Acorus calamus
Sweet flag root

Inula magnifica
Elecampane root

Elettaria cardamomum
Cardamom seeds

Pinus *sp.*
Large fir cone

Pinus *sp.*
Small fir cones

Cinnamomum zeylanicum
Cinnamon bark

Logwood chips

Quassia armara
Quassia chips

Myristica fragrans
Mace

Cedrus *sp.*
Cedar wood shavings

Pimenta dioica
Allspice

Populus candicans
Balm of Gilead buds

Carum carvi
Caraway seeds

Cedrus *sp.*
Cedar petals

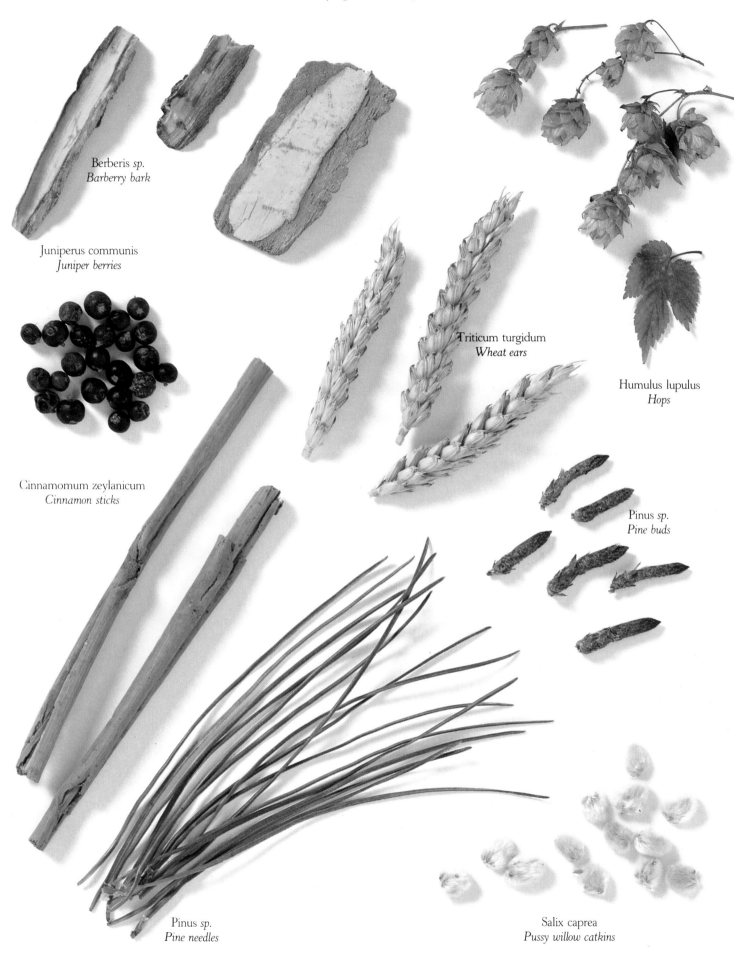

Berberis *sp.*
Barberry bark

Juniperus communis
Juniper berries

Cinnamomum zeylanicum
Cinnamon sticks

Triticum turgidum
Wheat ears

Humulus lupulus
Hops

Pinus *sp.*
Pine buds

Pinus *sp.*
Pine needles

Salix caprea
Pussy willow catkins

Aromatic fixatives

Fixatives play a key role in pot pourri: they absorb and retain the volatile scented oils that give the flowers, herbs, and other ingredients their perfume. If they were not used, a pot pourri would quickly lose its beautiful fragrance. Most fixatives are aromatic in themselves and add to the bouquet of a pot pourri as well as fixing its scent. A mix will usually call for at least two fixatives.

Fixative properties are found in certain gums, resins, roots, seeds, spices, herbs, woods, leaves, flowers, and even lichens. Orris root powder and gum benzoin are easiest to obtain and most commonly used, but cinnamon powder (or broken cinnamon sticks), cloves, and nutmeg are also effective fixatives and are usually to hand in the kitchen. Cumin and coriander can also be used but it is better to use the oil from these two fixatives. Sweet cicely seeds, angelica seeds, and chamomile flowers are all fixatives that can be grown in the garden, and the lovely grey lichen, known as oakmoss, which is an excellent and pretty fixative, can be found in England growing on trees, wooden fences, and gates. The soft, sweet odour of vanilla pods and tonquin, or tonka, beans will enhance the fragrance of a mix as well as hold its perfume. All the fixatives shown on these two pages are popular vegetable fixatives, which are easy to obtain. Others, which are not shown but which can easily be grown or obtained, include: the resins of myrrh, galbanum and labdanum; roots of spikenard, sweet flag, elecampane, and geranium; musk seed; oil of sandalwood, cassia, cedarwood, cypress, patchouli, ylang ylang, basil, marjoram, and thyme; and the leaves of sweet woodruff, melilot, myrtle, cistus, lemon verbena, and patchouli.

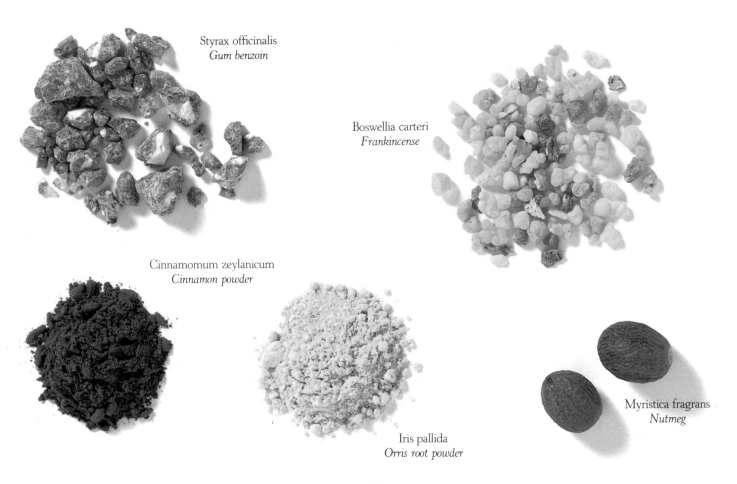

Styrax officinalis
Gum benzoin

Boswellia carteri
Frankincense

Cinnamomum zeylanicum
Cinnamon powder

Myristica fragrans
Nutmeg

Iris pallida
Orris root powder

Chamaemelum nobile
Chamomile flowers

Evernia purpuracea
Oakmoss

Syzygium aromaticum
Cloves

Myrrhis odorata
Sweet cicely seeds

Dipteryx odorata
Tonquin or tonka beans

Cuminum cyminum
Cumin seeds

Angelica archangelica
Angelica seeds

Coriandrum sativum
Coriander

Vanilla planifolia
Vanilla pod

Essential oils

*Extracted essential oils give pot pourri its strongest perfume. Just
a single oil or a combination of oils can be used, depending upon
what is available or appropriate to the recipe.*

*E*ssential oils are found in perfumed flowers, leaves,
roots, and even seeds. The buds of balsam poplar,
birch, cassia, cloves; and the flowers of pink and carnation,
heliotrope, honeysuckle, hyacinth, jasmine, jonquil, lilac,
lily-of-the-valley, orange blossom, rose, sweet pea, violet,
wallflower, and ylang ylang all contain essential oils. They
are also to be found in the leaves and stems of cinnamon,
patchouli, pelargonium, and vervain; and in the barks of
cassia, cedar, and cinnamon. The woods of cedar and
sandal, and the roots or rhizomes of sweet flag, ginger, iris
florentine, elecampane, geranium, angelica, sweet cicely,
roseroot, and some eryngiums contain essential oils; as do
citrus fruits, the seeds of cardamom, cumin, fennel, musk,
angelica, sweet cicely, nutmeg, and star anise, and the resins
of olibanum (frankincense), labdanum, myrrh, and storax.

The perfume of all these essential oils ranges from the
highly citric, through the floral and spicy, to the strong and
highly persistent aromas of wood, oakmoss, patchouli, iris,
and even the delicious vanilla.

Liberating perfumes

On a hot summer's day the air in the garden may be filled
with fragrance, for many flowers will release their perfume
freely in the heat of the sun. Other perfumes are liberated
when a plant is touched or bruised. Some leaves, roots, and
seeds have to be crushed, however, to liberate (or discharge)
the scent contained within them.

To obtain an essential oil for use in perfumery, it is
necessary to separate it from the plant material by any one
of the following three methods: expression, distillation, or
extraction. In the first, pressure is applied to the plant
material to squeeze out the oil: citrus fruit oils are obtained in
this manner. In the distillation process, fragrant material is
placed in boiling water, so that when the essential oil
evaporates, it mixes with the steam from the water. Then,
when the steam condenses, the oil separates from the water
and floats on the surface.

Extracting essential oils

Extraction involves the infusion of the fragrant plant material in fat, oil, or spirit. There are two ways of extracting
essential oils. In the first – *enfleurage* – the fragrant plant
material is infused in cool olive oil. When the fragrant oils
have been released into the olive oil, the exhausted flowers
and petals are removed and replaced with fresh ones. Flowers and oil are most easily separated by straining the oil,
pressing the flowers down firmly. This process is repeated
until the oil is saturated with perfume. In the second method
of extraction – maceration – the oil is heated to cause the
perfumes to be more readily given up by the fragrant
materials. The container of oil is placed in a pan of hot water
for a few hours and the plant material changed daily until the
oil is saturated with fragrance as before.

The essential oils that I use most frequently are the
traditional rose and lavender oils, which are appropriate for
so many recipes. However, experiment with different oils to
discover the combinations of scented flowers and perfume
you prefer. Try making some essential oils yourself by
extracting them, using the *enfleurage* or maceration
methods, which are both easy to do at home.

Lavender oil

Frankincense

Rose oil

Patchouli oil

Bergamot oil

MAKING A MOIST POT POURRI

1 To make the stock-pot, place a 1cm- (½ in-) layer of partially dried rose petals in a storage container. Sprinkle over the top some coarse salt (a third of the thickness of the petals). Add a second layer of petals and press down firmly with your hand. Spoon on top another layer of salt.

2 Sprinkle a pinch of brown sugar and a few drops of brandy on this and every subsequent second layer of petals and salt. Continue layering with petals, salt, sugar, and brandy until the container is full. Seal and leave to cure for two months. Check and drain if necessary.

3 Crumble the cured cake of rose petals or stock-pot into a bowl containing the spices, herbs, fixatives, and essential oils required by the recipe. Mix thoroughly and allow to cure for a further three weeks. Transfer to a bowl and decorate or to a lidded, perforated pot-pourri dish.

Rose petals

Salt

Sugar

Storage container

Spoon

Brandy

Mixing bowl

Stock-pot

Scent on Show

This chapter contains twenty recipes of many different scents and appearances. There are chintzy mixes with floral fragrances; pretty herby pot pourris, smelling of lemon or mint; hauntingly rich moist mixes; traditional damask rose bowls of rich blooms; and many other tantalizing recipes. In each recipe you will find five main groups of ingredients: the fragrant flowers and petals, the herbs, the spices, the fixatives, and the essential oils. Every pot pourri contains material from each of these groups. The quantities I have given will fill a medium-sized mixing bowl. Pot pourri can be made using one of two methods: the dry method (see p.72) and the moist method (see p.87). I have included many more recipes that call for the dry method, as it is far easier to make pot pourri by this means, and the results are much more attractive visually. However, a good moist mix has an unsurpassed fragrance, and I have included a few recipes under "Heady Aromas".

ROSE AND
SCENTED-LEAF GERANIUM POT POURRI

1 litre (1 quart) rose petals and blooms
50g (2oz) scented geranium (pelargonium) leaves
25g (1oz) rosemary
25g (1oz) orris root powder
½ teaspoon whole cloves
½ teaspoon ground allspice
½ teaspoon grated nutmeg
3 drops rose oil
1 drop rosemary oil
1 drop geranium oil
rose blooms to decorate

*A slightly spicy, traditional rose recipe decorated with rose blooms.
The perfumes of the geranium leaves and rosemary lend a
sharpness to the overall aroma.*

ROSE AND
GARDEN-FLOWER POT POURRI

500ml (1 pint) rose petals and blooms
500ml (1 pint) mixed garden flowers
25g (1oz) lavender
50g (2oz) mixed sweet herbs
25g (1oz) orris root powder
2 level teaspoons cinnamon powder
½ teaspoon whole cloves
2 star anise
3 drops rose oil
2 drops carnation oil
2 drops lemon oil

*Roses and other garden flowers combine to create a fresh floral pot
pourri lighter in bouquet than an all-rose mix.*

❧ ROSE AND MINT POT POURRI ❧

1 litre (1 quart) rose petals and blooms
25g (1oz) mint leaves
25g (1oz) lavender
25g (1oz) orris root powder
½ teaspoon whole cloves
1 teaspoon cinnamon powder
½ teaspoon ground mace
3 drops rose oil
2 drops rosewood oil
1 drop lemon oil

*A sweet rose pot pourri with the refreshing influence of mint. The
mint has a distinctive aroma that contrasts beautifully with the
delicate perfume of the rose petals.*

❧ EASY SWEET-HERB MIX ❧

1 litre (1 quart) mixed sweet herbs
25g (1oz) lavender
25g (1oz) orris root powder
2 teaspoons cinnamon powder
½ teaspoon whole cloves
3 drops lavender oil
3 drops lemon oil
flowers to decorate

A lavendery, sweet-herb pot pourri with a hint of lemon.

❧ SPICY HERB MIX ❧

1 litre (1 quart) mixed lemon verbena, eau-de-Cologne mint,
elecampane leaves, bergamot, and basil
50g (2oz) scented geranium leaves
25g (1oz) lavender
25g (1oz) orris root powder
2 teaspoons cinnamon powder
½ teaspoon ground allspice
½ teaspoon grated nutmeg
½ teaspoon caraway seeds
3 drops bergamot oil
3 drops geranium oil
flowers to decorate

A rich, aromatic herb pot pourri decorated formally.

❧ PEPPERMINT MIX ❧

500ml (1 pint) peppermint leaves
500ml (1 pint) mixed eau-de-Cologne mint, thyme,
costmary, and sweet cicely leaves
50g (2oz) rosemary
25g (1oz) lavender
25g (1oz) orris root powder
½ teaspoon ground allspice
½ teaspoon whole cloves
½ teaspoon grated nutmeg
2 pieces cinnamon bark
2 drops peppermint oil
2 drops basil oil
1 drop lemon oil
flowers to decorate

*A charming pot pourri with a spicy peppermint fragrance that
will keep the kitchen smelling deliciously fresh.*

WILD-MINT AND SWEET-BRIAR MIX

500ml (1 pint) mixed sweet-briar leaves and blossom
500ml (1 pint) mixed wild mints
25g (1oz) marjoram
25g (1oz) lavender
25g (1oz) orris root powder
½ teaspoon whole cloves
½ teaspoon grated nutmeg
2 teaspoons cinnamon powder
1 drop lavender oil
1 drop peppermint oil
3 drops rose oil
flowers to decorate

A mixture with a delightful rose scent and a hint of mint.

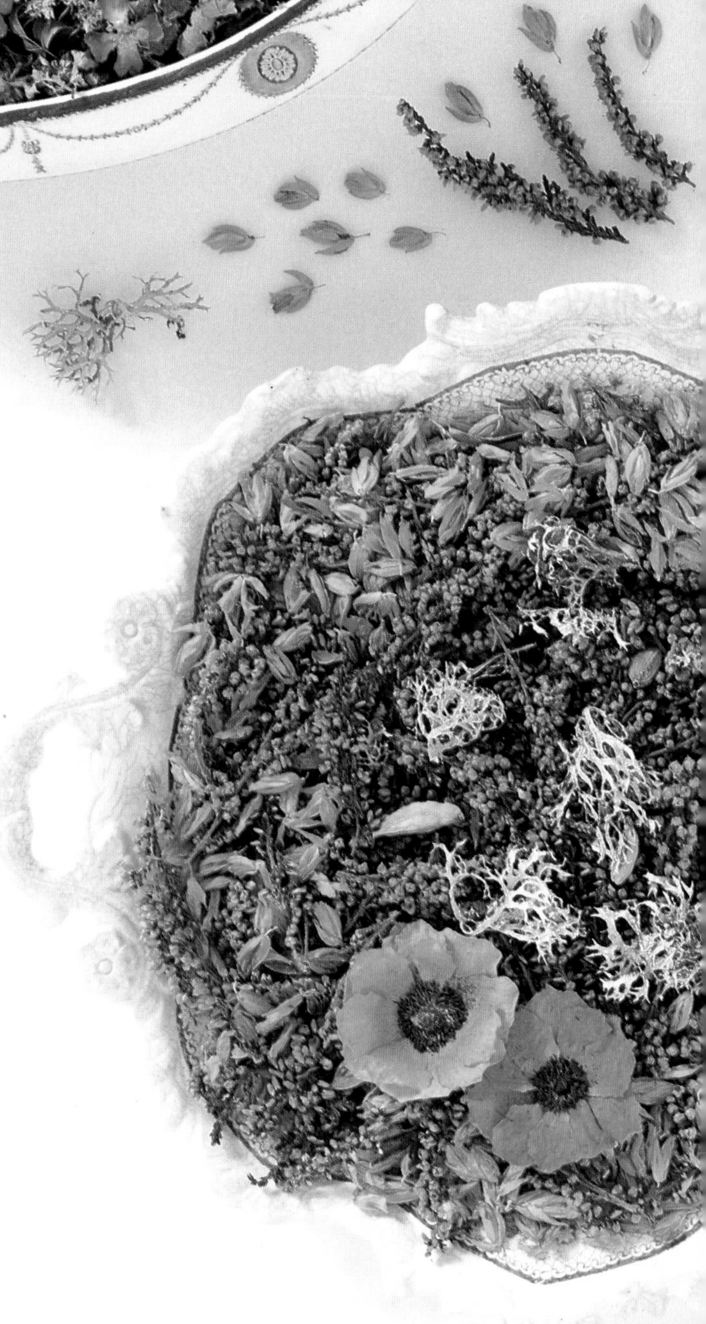

HEATHER- AND GORSE-FLOWER MIX

1 litre (1 quart) mixed heather and gorse flowers
50g (2oz) oakmoss (or lavender)
25g (1oz) orris root powder
2 teaspoons cinnamon powder
½ teaspoon ground cloves
3 crushed cardamoms
2 drops lavender oil
2 drops rose oil
1 drop almond essence
flowers to decorate

A traditional floral fragrance with a hint of almond.

❧ WOODRUFF MIX ❧

1 litre (1 quart) mixed flowers, comprising three or more of the following: honeysuckle, burnet rose, gorse, elder flower, lily-of-the-valley, sweet violet, fleabane, and St. John's wort
50g (2oz) woodruff
50g (2oz) melilot (or another 50g/2oz woodruff)
25g (1oz) costmary
25g (1oz) orris root powder
2 blades ground mace
1 crushed tonquin bean
½ teaspoon grated nutmeg
½ teaspoon ground allspice
3 drops rose, violet or lily-of-the-valley oil
3 drops lavender oil
flowers to decorate

A rich and slightly musky floral pot pourri. This mix of yellows, pinks, and greens also looks very effective in a small wooden bowl or unsophisticated wicker basket.

OLD-FASHIONED
⚜ MIXED-FLOWER POT POURRI ⚜

1 litre (1 quart) mixed flowers from the following: rose,
honeysuckle, violet, pink, larkspur, lemon verbena, cornflower,
and wallflower
50g (2oz) mixed sweet herbs
25g (1oz) lavender
25g (1oz) orris root powder
25g (1oz) fine-ground gum benzoin
½ teaspoon whole cloves
½ teaspoon ground allspice
½ cinnamon stick
2 drops rose oil
2 drops carnation oil
1 drop lemon oil
1 drop frankincense
flowers to decorate

A mixture of scented flowers and sweet herbs lends a rich, flowery
fragrance to this old-fashioned pot pourri.

SWEET-HERB AND ROSE-BUD POT POURRI

500ml (1 pint) rose petals and buds
500ml (1 pint) mixed bergamot, sweet cicely leaves, marjoram,
lemon verbena, bay leaves,
and angelica leaves
25g (1oz) lavender
25g (1oz) orris root powder
2 teaspoons cinnamon powder
½ teaspoon angelica seeds
½ teaspoon whole cloves
½ teaspoon ground mace
½ teaspoon grated nutmeg
3 drops rose oil
2 drops bergamot oil
1 drop frankincense
flowers to decorate

*The herbs and rose petals, together with a hint of frankincense,
make this pot pourri richly aromatic.*

PRETTY VICTORIAN POT POURRI

500ml (1 pint) mixed pink, mauve or cream, scented material
from the following: rose buds, violet, pink, chamomile flowers,
and heliotrope
500ml (1 pint) mixed thyme, rosemary, myrtle, sweet cicely
leaves, and bergamot
25g (1oz) lavender
25g (1oz) orris root powder
25g (1oz) fine-ground gum benzoin
½ cinnamon stick
½ teaspoon whole cloves
½ teaspoon ground allspice
2 drops rose oil
2 drops lavender oil
2 drops lemon oil
pink and mauve flowers to decorate

*The prettiest, nostalgic Victorian pot pourri with the sweet smell of
old-fashioned flowers.*

MARIGOLD, LEMON AND MINT MIX

500ml (1 pint) mixed marigold and chamomile flowers
500ml (1 pint) mixed lemon balm and mint
50g (2oz) lavender
25g (1oz) rosemary
25g (1oz) orris root powder
½ cinnamon stick
1 strip lemon peel
½ teaspoon whole cloves
½ teaspoon grated nutmeg
3 drops geranium oil
2 drops lemon oil
1 drop peppermint oil
flowers to decorate (parsley, anaphalis and blue larkspur)

*A sharp, fresh pot pourri. The bold orange of the marigold flowers
makes this mix quite vibrant.*

FRAGRANT-ROOT POT POURRI

500ml (1 pint) mixed, chopped root, comprising at least three
of the following: geranium, roseroot, angelica, elecampane,
sweet flag, sweet cicely, and herb bennet
25g (1oz) lavender
25g (1oz) orris root powder
½ teaspoon whole cloves
½ teaspoon ground allspice
2 blades ground mace
25g (1oz) quassia chips
peel of a lime
4 drops rose oil
2 drops sandalwood oil
mock orange flowers to decorate

*A different style of pot pourri with a refined and musky perfume
and highly textural appearance.*

✣ HERB AND LAVENDER MIX ✣

1 litre (1 quart) mixed woodruff,
rosemary, bergamot, and
elecampane leaves
75g (2½oz) lavender
25g (1oz) orris root powder
½ cinnamon stick
½ teaspoon ground cloves
½ teaspoon grated nutmeg
3 drops lavender oil
3 drops bergamot oil
flowers to decorate

A soft and sweet-smelling pot pourri that looks just right in an unobtrusive rustic basket.

99

❧ YELLOW AND ORANGE MIX ❧

1 litre (1 quart) petals and blooms in shades of yellow
and orange
50g (2oz) mixed sweet herbs
25g (1oz) orris root powder
25g (1oz) lavender
2 teaspoons cinnamon powder
½ teaspoon grated nutmeg
½ teaspoon whole cloves
a few pieces lemon and orange peel
3 drops lemon oil
3 drops geranium oil

*Sweet-smelling herbs and yellow and orange flowers in a piquant,
lemony pot pourri.*

100

❧ WHITE AND CREAM MIX ❧

1 litre (1 quart) petals and blooms in shades of
white and cream
50g (2oz) mixed sweet herbs
25g (1oz) rosemary
25g (1oz) orris root powder
2 teaspoons fine-ground gum benzoin
3 crushed cardamoms
½ teaspoon whole cloves
2 drops geranium oil
2 drops rosewood oil
1 drop lemon oil

*This unusual mixture of white flowers and herbs has a
charming, lingering sweet smell.*

❧ BLUE AND MAUVE MIX ❧

1 litre (1 quart) petals and blooms in shades of blue and mauve
50g (2oz) mixed grey-leaved sweet herbs
25g (1oz) lavender
25g (1oz) orris root powder
½ teaspoon whole cloves
½ teaspoon ground allspice
3 blades ground mace
3 drops lavender oil
2 drops bergamot oil

*Delft-blue flowers mixed with grey-leaved sweet herbs make a
charming pot pourri with a lavender fragrance.*

❧ SWEET FLORAL POT POURRI ❧

1 litre (1 quart) crumbled stock-pot petals
25g (1oz) lavender
12g (½oz) fine-ground gum benzoin
25g (1oz) orris root powder
½ chopped vanilla pod
1 teaspoon crushed cardamom
½ teaspoon ground cloves

½ teaspoon grated nutmeg
1 drop frankincense
2 drops lavender oil
3 drops rose oil
flowers to decorate if required

A rich and sweet, flowery pot pourri. Decorate the mix with flowers or keep in a lidded container. Here, dried rich-red and pink rose and potentilla flowers empathize with the translucent pink dish.

ROSE, PHILADELPHUS, AND CARNATION MIX

1 litre (1 quart) mixed fresh rose petals, fresh mock orange
blossom, and fresh clove carnation or pink flowers
50g (2oz) mixed fresh mint, fresh marjoram, and
fresh rosemary
50g (2oz) lavender
4 bay leaves
25g (1oz) cinnamon powder
½ teaspoon ground cloves
lavender water (sprinkling)
brandy (sprinkling)
12g (½oz) fine-ground gum benzoin
½ teaspoon grated nutmeg
12g (½oz) orris root powder
100g (4oz) bay salt (not table salt)

*An ancient recipe for a moist pot pourri, which is made differently
from other moist mixes in that all the ingredients are mixed
together and layered in a jar with the salt, brandy and lavender
water. The jar is then sealed and the contents left to cure for two
months, stirring daily. This tall glass jar was layered with dried
flowers, herbs, and spices, and a muslin bag filled with the matured
pot pourri was buried inside.*

LEMON MIX

1 litre (1 quart) crumbled stock-pot petals
25g (1oz) lavender
50g (2oz) mixed lemon balm and lemon verbena
25g (1oz) lemon-scented geranium leaves
25g (1oz) rosemary
crushed peel of ¼ lemon
25g (1oz) orris root powder
½ teaspoon cinnamon powder
½ teaspoon ground cloves
3 drops lemon oil
2 drops rose oil
1 drop lavender oil
flowers to decorate if required

*A very lemony and piquant pot pourri. Here, dried rose petals and
blooms decorate the mix when the lid is removed.*

SCENT AROUND THE HOUSE

For thousands of years fragrant flowers, leaves, roots, seeds, woods and resins have been used to scent our homes, food, clothes as well as ourselves. As we gradually became aware of the soothing and sybaritic properties of perfume, more sophisticated mans were found to capture the many aromas of the natural world.

It was probably the scented smoke of burning wood that first alerted our senses to the pleasure of perfume for the word "perfume" is derived from *per fumin*, meaning "by means of smoke". The Greek and Roman civilizations of the ancient Western world gained their knowledge of perfumery from the Egyptians. In the eleventh century, the Arabian doctor Avicenna perfected the science of distillation, and the Crusaders brought many exquisitely perfumed toiletries and exciting new aromatics back from the eastern Mediterranean.

By the sixteenth century most large houses grew herbs and scented flowers – particularly roses – in their gardens. They were gathered by the mistress of the house and taken to her "still-room" – a room apart from the kitchen where a stove kept the atmosphere warm and dry. They were dried and stored there together with the many imported herbs and spices that were available. Oils, fats and lards, lanolin, beeswax and precious animal fixatives added to the fascinating contents of the room. One can imagine the delectable and curious scents that filled the air. Hence the housewife dispensed all the cosmetics, cleaners and medicines that were essential to the well-being of her family and the sweetness of her home.

Large bundles of herbs were prepared for strewing on the floors and fumigating the rooms. Scented pastilles and incense cones were made to sweeten the air, as were rich moist pot pourris. Fragrant and moth-repellent fillings were made for sachets, which were then used to perfume and protect clothes and linen. Aromatic pomanders and spikenard, rosemary and essential oils; they perfumed the air and their germicidal properties helped to ward off infection. Delicately scented washballs, soaps, colognes, floral waters, oils and other preparations were made for cosmetic use.

This section contains both traditional and innovative ways of perfuming every room in the house. Some of the fragrant delights are steeped in antiquity, whilst others are my own ideas.

BASIC TECHNIQUES

❊

THE TECHNIQUES USED to make all the fragrant delights in this section are quite simple to follow and, once you have mastered them you can become more ambitious in the things you create. It is best to begin by learning how to make both dry and moist pot pourris, for, in doing so, you will understand the fundamental rules of creating and holding a fragrance. Pot pourri consists of five main groups of elements. First come the dried botanicals that form the bulk of the mix. In a dry pot pourri these might be rose petals or other scented petals or flowers, leaves, roots, seeds

❊ EXTRACTING PERFUMES *Drying leaves and flowers or making scented oils above are just two ways of using the fragrant elements in plants.*

or woods; sometimes this group consists of dried botanicals that are attractive but not scented. In a moist pot pourri rose petals are cured with salt (and possibly brown sugar and brandy too). The resulting "stock pot" makes up the first group of botanicals. Second come the complementary sweet herbs. Usually just lavender is used although rosemary and other herbs can be included. Third come the fixatives. I have used mainly orris root powder or fine-ground gum benzoin. Fixatives are essential for holding the fragrance and without them the pot pourri quickly loses its scent. Fourth come the spices which add a subtle and interesting depth to the bouquet of the mix. Finally come the essential oils, the perfume of which dominates the pot pourri. Essential oils are concentrated perfumes extracted from aromatic plant materials. You will also need some lovely whole flowers and leaves, and possibly some whole spices, in order to decorate the whole mix. Scented colognes, essences, waters and oils are made by immersing fragrant plant materials in alcohol, vinegar or oil, this extracts the perfume from them.

❊

✦ FRESH FLOWERS ❧

Brighten and perfume any room in the house by decorating it with fresh, scented flowers and aromatic greenery.

Gather the fragrant plant materials when the sun has dried the dew on them but has not yet made the delicate flowers wilt: this is usually around midday. Choose flowers and leaves that are in good condition; if they are damaged they will quickly deteriorate and you will have to renew the display.

Start by making a simple, fan-shaped arrangement, such as the one shown here, and then experiment with other shapes as your confidence grows.

1 *Gather the tools and ingredients you need: a knife to cut the wet foam, scissors or secateurs to trim stems and leaves, an attractive container and the plant materials.*

2 *Shape the foam to fit the container. Place it inside and moisten it well. Starting from the centre back, make a basic fan shape. Then fill out towards the front.*

❀ Winter Greenery
This display of scented evergreens, with fragrant jonquils and daphne to provide colour, is arranged in a classic fan shape.

⋅ DECORATED CANDLES ⋅

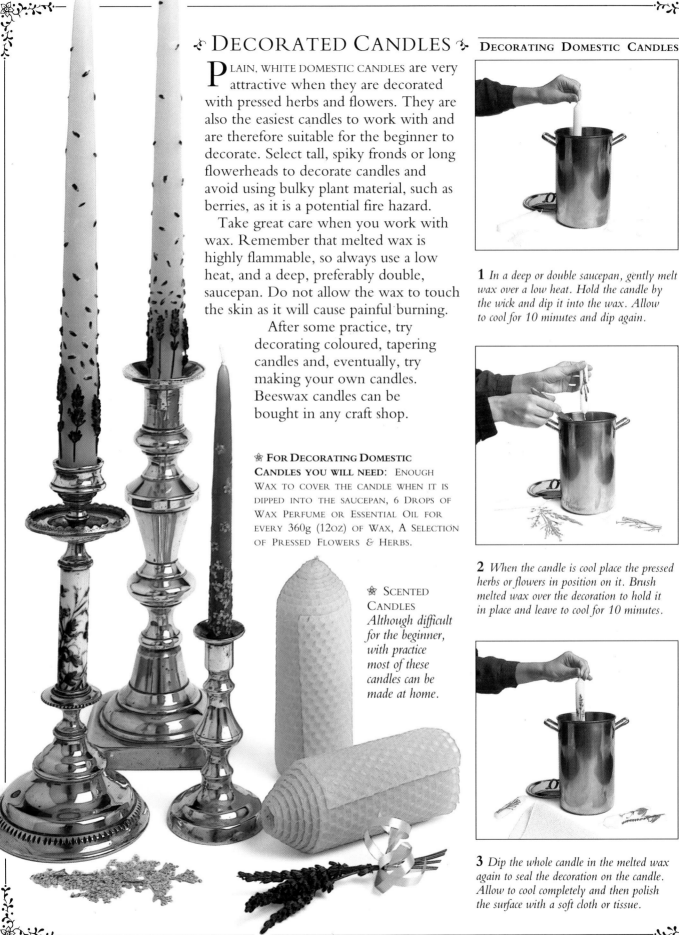

PLAIN, WHITE DOMESTIC CANDLES are very attractive when they are decorated with pressed herbs and flowers. They are also the easiest candles to work with and are therefore suitable for the beginner to decorate. Select tall, spiky fronds or long flowerheads to decorate candles and avoid using bulky plant material, such as berries, as it is a potential fire hazard.

Take great care when you work with wax. Remember that melted wax is highly flammable, so always use a low heat, and a deep, preferably double, saucepan. Do not allow the wax to touch the skin as it will cause painful burning.

After some practice, try decorating coloured, tapering candles and, eventually, try making your own candles. Beeswax candles can be bought in any craft shop.

❀ **FOR DECORATING DOMESTIC CANDLES YOU WILL NEED:** ENOUGH WAX TO COVER THE CANDLE WHEN IT IS DIPPED INTO THE SAUCEPAN, 6 DROPS OF WAX PERFUME OR ESSENTIAL OIL FOR EVERY 360g (12OZ) OF WAX, A SELECTION OF PRESSED FLOWERS & HERBS.

❀ SCENTED CANDLES *Although difficult for the beginner, with practice most of these candles can be made at home.*

1 *In a deep or double saucepan, gently melt wax over a low heat. Hold the candle by the wick and dip it into the wax. Allow to cool for 10 minutes and dip again.*

2 *When the candle is cool place the pressed herbs or flowers in position on it. Brush melted wax over the decoration to hold it in place and leave to cool for 10 minutes.*

3 *Dip the whole candle in the melted wax again to seal the decoration on the candle. Allow to cool completely and then polish the surface with a soft cloth or tissue.*

❧ CUSHIONS & SACHETS ❧

LARGE, SCENTED CUSHIONS are easy to make and, once you have mastered the basic sewing techniques, smaller, more intricate, fragrant sachets will be well within your abilities.

Cushion covers are best made from materials that can be removed and washed, especially if the cushions will be in frequent use. Sachets are usually used purely as decoration so they can be made of more delicate materials, such as ribbon and lace.

❀ **FOR SACHETS & CUSHIONS YOU WILL NEED:** SCISSORS, PINS, NEEDLE, THREAD, CLOTH, LACE, RIBBON, WADDING, POT POURRI.

MAKING A CUSHION

1 *Use a template to cut out 6 pieces of 120g (4oz), flame-proof wadding. The shape should be 1cm ($^1/_2$ in) smaller all-round than the cover you intend to use.*

2 *Holding or pinning the 6 pieces of wadding together, sew around 3 sides of the shape, to make an envelope. (If the shape is round, leave a portion of the edge unsewn.)*

3 *Fill the wadding envelope with a highly scented pot pourri. Sew the final edge together. Cut out and sew around 3 sides of the material you wish to use as a cover.*

❀ CUSHIONS
*Large, scented
cushions require
more sewing than
sachets but are less
fiddly to make.*

❀ BUTTERFLIES
*Sachets can be any
shape. These butterflies
are simple to make and
quite charming.*

4 *Ease the envelope of wadding into the
cushion cover and sew up the final edge.
(Use poppers or a zip if you wish to be
able to remove the filling at a later date.)*

❧ SCENTED PAPER ❧

SCENTED STATIONERY is simple to make and adds a special touch to your correspondence. Make stationery using art paper, tearing it by hand to give it an attractive edge, or decorate shop-bought paper. Scent the paper by storing it with a sachet of pot pourri for four weeks. Perfume and protect pressed-flower designs on bookmarks, gift tags and cards by painting them with melted, scented wax.

TEARING & SCENTING PAPER

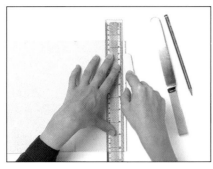

1 *Use a ruler to draw a line where you wish to tear the paper. Score line with a knife, fold and press along the fold. Turn paper over and repeat. Tear paper along the fold.*

2 *Staple together 2 tissues or nappy liners on 3 sides to make a sachet. Fill it with pot pourri and staple the final edge. Place the sachet and paper in a plastic bag and seal.*

❀ PAPER ARRAY *A wide variety of stationery can be made at home.*

❀ BLUE PAPER *Stored in a plastic bag with a pot-pourri sachet, this paper is imbued with scent.*

❀ CITRUS POMANDER
The tangy scent of a citrus pomander is especially lovely in the kitchen.

❀ **FOR A FLORAL POMANDER YOU WILL NEED:** A SPHERE OF DRY FOAM, 60g (2oz) OF LAVENDER FLOWERS, A GOOD SELECTION OF SCENTED, DRIED FLOWERS, GLUE, RIBBON.

❀ **FOR A CITRUS POMANDER YOU WILL NEED:** A CITRUS FRUIT, CLOVES, 30g (1oz) ORRIS ROOT POWDER, 30g (1oz) CINNAMON POWDER, 4 DROPS OF A TANGY ESSENTIAL OIL, TAPE, RIBBON, PINS, BEADS, A KNITTING NEEDLE.

❀ FLORAL POMANDER
Brighten and scent any room with a floral pomander.

⚜ POMANDERS ⚜

THERE ARE TWO basic types of pomander: the citrus pomander – a citrus fruit decorated with cloves – and the floral pomander – a sphere of dry foam decorated with dried flowers. Although time-consuming, neither type is difficult to learn how to make and the end result is a lovely, scented decoration.

MAKING A FLORAL POMANDER

1 *Using a paintbrush, dab patches of glue on to the dry foam then carefully roll it in the lavender flowers.*

2 *Using tweezers, pick up a dried flower, dip the back into glue, then place in position. Add flowers of a kind in small groups.*

MAKING A CITRUS POMANDER

1 *Divide the fruit into quarters with tape. Starting next to the tape, working into the centre of each quarter, make holes ³/₄cm (¹/₃ in) apart. Place a clove in each hole.*

2 *Remove tape and put the pomander in a bag containing a mixture of cinnamon, orris root and essential oil. Shake well, remove, brush off excess and wrap in tissue paper.*

3 *Leave in a dry place for 2 to 3 weeks. Remove from tissue. Decorate with ribbon and beads. (Omit step 2 should you wish to have a purely citrus-scented pomander.)*

❧ DECORATIONS ❧

One of the most beautiful and effective ways of using dried flowers is in a three-dimensional design. Such a decoration looks wonderful displayed in the centre of a table but, of course, you can place them on many other flat surfaces to great effect.

The basic steps to follow are straightforward but the finished arrangement can be as intricate as you wish. Begin with a simple design and then experiment with more ambitious ideas.

MAKING A CENTREPIECE

3 *When the moss is in place, turn over the card and glue a border of lacy flowers on the underside. They should extend over the edge so that they are visible from the right side.*

1 *With a pencil, mark your design on to watercolour paper or white card. Use a template if you wish. Then cut carefully around the shape, using sharp scissors.*

4 *Trim any stalks off the flowers. Starting from the outside, gradually work inwards, gluing the flowers on to the moss in informal rows that follow the shape of the card.*

2 *Cover the whole of the shape with moss. Pick up the pieces of moss with tweezers, dip the backs into a saucer of glue and then stick them in place on the card.*

5 *Add scent by carefully dripping essential oil followed by oil of cloves into the centre of a few of the flowers. Oil of cloves is a fixative, so the perfume will be long-lasting.*

❧ TOILETRIES ❧

Cosmetic creams, perfumes, soaps, shampoos, bath oils and toilet waters are very simple to make in your own home. Most of the ingredients involved are natural and you can scent the products with your favourite fragrances. Food colouring can be added to alcohol- or vinegar-based toiletries to make them more visually attractive.

❀ FOR JONQUIL COLOGNE YOU WILL NEED: 500ml (1pt) VODKA, A SUPPLY OF FRESH, HIGHLY PERFUMED JONQUILS, 2 DROPS OF FOOD COLOURING.

❀ FOR BODY OIL YOU WILL NEED: 50ml (1½ fl oz) ALMOND OIL, 10 DROPS OF ANY FLORAL ESSENTIAL OIL.

✤ SCENTED DELIGHTS
*All these cosmetics
and toiletries can be
made at home.*

MAKING JONQUIL COLOGNE

MAKING BODY OIL

1 *Pour in enough vodka to reach the shoulders of a bottle. Push the flowers into the bottle until the liquid is full. Cork and leave for 10 days, gently shaking daily.*

2 *Strain the liquid and replace the flowers with new ones. Repeat the whole process 3 times then bottle, add colouring and cork. Use glue to attach dried-flower decorations.*

This is one of the easiest toiletries to make. Pour almond oil into a bottle, add essential oil, place the stopper in the bottle and shake well. The oil is now ready to use.

THE HALL & STAIRS

THE HALL SETS THE SCENE for the entire home, and what could be more welcoming than a seductive fragrance. On entering the visitor immediately searches for the source of the perfume and derives much pleasure from the discovery of a basket or bowl brimming with pot pourri, or an aromatic garland behind the door or looped over the newel post of the stairs. There are many garland bases available and when they are decorated with dried flowers, leaves, fruit, whole spices, mosses and lichen, their romantic charm always adds interest to any interior. Pretty old hats and bonnets, stuffed with sweet herbs and flowers, are a delightful decoration. One used to be able to obtain scented pictures from the East, with hollow frames which were filled with spicy aromatics. Although these are no longer available you can easily

❀ GARLANDS & COLLAGES *Unusual garlands (left) and delicately-scented collages (above) are wonderful decorations for the hall and stairs.*

recreate them by rubbing wooden picture frames with the essential oil of cloves, cinnamon, nutmeg, sandalwood or cedarwood. Gentle, subtle perfumes are best for the hall and stairs as they will not spread to overwhelm the scents in other rooms. Colours should be warm and welcoming. The browns of woods and spices and the subdued pinks, mauves and blues of cottage garden flowers are ideal. Aromatic woods can often be collected on a woodland walk. Fir needles are easily discovered as are conifer foliage and fir cones, the refreshing scent of which can be strengthened by dropping a little pine oil into their centres. Sharpen woody scents with the intriguing perfume of bergamot orange. The shadowy fragrance of the rose is always welcome. Mix it with sweet herbs to produce a very lovely traditional fragrance.

❧ FLORAL HOOPS ❧

Consider carefully the colours and scents to use in your floral decorations for the hall, as they will be the first decorations a visitor to your house will encounter and they are therefore bound to make a significant impression. Shades of brown and green and woody or spicy scents are ideal as they empathize with the world outside, so close at hand. If you have also made pot pourris for the hall, ensure that their scents and colours complement those of the garlands. In addition to the wall, you might also like to hang a garland on the newel at the end of the banisters or on the inner side of the front door. Enhance or refresh the scent of a garland by rubbing perfumed oil into the willow base or by periodically spraying the base or the flowers with perfume.

LILAC

POTENTILLA

❀ SEMI BASKET *Flowers and other plant materials, scented with essential oils and glued to a cardboard backing, produce a fine display for this two-dimensional garland.*

EVERLASTING FLOWERS

ROSE

❀ MOSSY GARLAND
*Browns, creams, greys
and greens are used to
give this garland a
muted appearance. A
lovely scent is produced
by the sandalwood oil, which
has been dropped on the
oakmoss and the pine cones,
and the whole spices.*

FIR CONE

CINNAMON STICK

WHEAT EAR

NUTMEG

❀ DELICATE CIRCLET
*Rose oil and myrrh oil
have been dropped into
the centre of each of
the roses to imbue this
dainty circlet with a
wonderful perfume
that is both ancient
and evocative.*

SEA CARROT

GLOBE AMARANTH

❧ FLORAL WALL HANGINGS ❧

THE LARGE AREA OF WALL SPACE in the hall and by the side of the stairs is ideal for the display of hanging scented decorations. Eye-catching arrangements for these positions can take almost any form you like. Try decorating objects that are usually found in the hall, such as the coat rack or the umbrella stand, or make just one bold design that will act as a focal point. As the hall and stairs are generally quite airy, make the scent fairly strong but not so powerful that it spreads throughout the rest of the house and overwhelms the perfumes in other rooms. Woody scents are very effective or, for a refreshing fragrance, try mixing citrus peel and herbs.

❀ HEART OF HOPS
& HEATHER
*Visually stunning,
although simple in
design, this rich
purple and pale green
heart is scented with a
pot-pourri reviver.*

❀ POSY OF PRESSED FLOWERS *This tiny, pressed-flower bouquet is bordered with a gilt frame. The back of the frame has been rubbed with oil of cloves, so that the picture exudes a strong but simple fragrance.*

❀ EDWARDIAN HAT *Decorated with dried flowers and filled with pot pourri, this lovely hat exudes the rich fragrance of scented woods and bergamot orange.*

The Living Room

Of all the rooms in the house, the living room is the best place to display your most lavish perfumed achievements. Pressed-flower pictures, using the scented flowers of a summer garden or an array of old roses, surrounded by a mixed border of flowers, are lovely. Use scented paper as a base or perfume the flowers so that the air around the collage is infused with fragrance. If you have the space, a large basket filled with fascinating aromatics might make the most intriguing feature in the room. Be imaginative when displaying pot pourri. Bowls, jars, dishes and baskets of fragrant mixes can be placed almost anywhere. Create immense impact by filling an old wooden rocking cradle, a chest or a dough bin with a magnificent display of dried roses, peonies, tulips and any other rich and flamboyant flowers. Make appliqué and

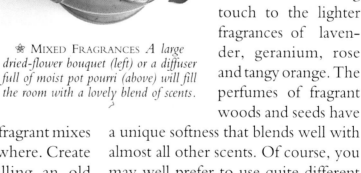

❀ MIXED FRAGRANCES *A large dried-flower bouquet (left) or a diffuser full of moist pot pourri (above) will fill the room with a lovely blend of scents.*

patchwork cushions and sachets from scraps of fabric and lace, or create frilled and piped cushions from a fabric that matches or co-ordinates with the other soft furnishings in the room. If the fragrant delights are to be displayed over a large area, scent them with different mixes, although be careful not to make them too overpowering. Just a little myrrh frankincense or patchouli will add a rich and soothing touch to the lighter fragrances of lavender, geranium, rose and tangy orange. The perfumes of fragrant woods and seeds have a unique softness that blends well with almost all other scents. Of course, you may well prefer to use quite different perfumes in your living room than those suggested. It is all a matter of personal choice, and you can have great fun experimenting to discover what appeals most.

❧ CUSHIONS ❧

SWEETLY PERFUMED cushions are a delightful way to scent the living room. Use pretty scraps of linen, lace and fabric to make opulent appliqué cushions or more humble patchwork ones – whichever suits the room. Fabrics that co-ordinate with other soft furnishings are also appropriate. Choice of scent is highly personal and can vary from light perfumes to luxuriant aromas.

❀ PATCHWORK & APPLIQUE
These lightly scented, hand-worked cushions are ideal for cottagey rooms.

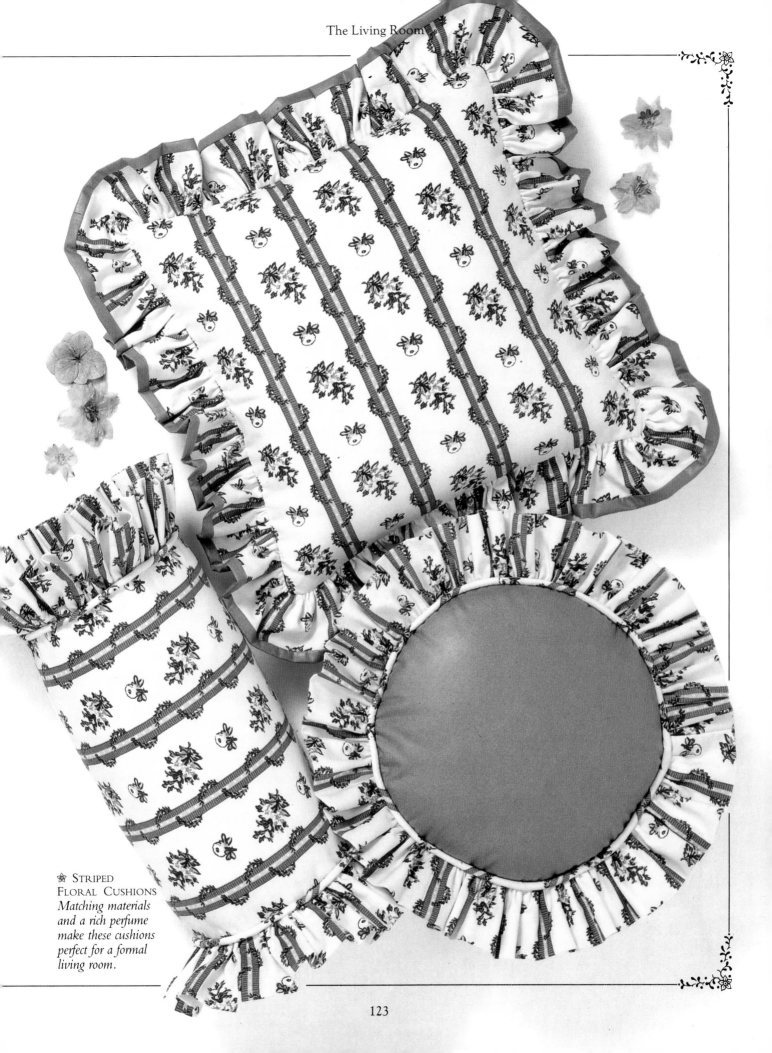

❋ STRIPED
FLORAL CUSHIONS
*Matching materials
and a rich perfume
make these cushions
perfect for a formal
living room.*

✌ SCENTED STATIONERY ✌

PRESSED FLOWERS, glue and good-quality art paper are all that you require to make your own unique and charming cards, notelets, note paper, envelopes, bookmarks and gift tags. Perfume your stationery by storing it in a small box or a drawer along with a sachet of pot pourri. Choose one of your favourite scents to perfume the paper and alter it whenever the mood takes you. Bookmarks can be scented with woodruff, which is an insect-repellent and is a time-honoured protector of paper. Scent your inks with a fragrant infusion – the traditional perfume is patchouli – for a personal touch to your letters.

❀ PEN & INK
*Scent your ink
with heady
patchouli.*

❀ CARDS & NOTELETS
*These beautiful cards are
imbued with the scent
of a lavender sachet
and decorated with
pressed flowers.*

❀ WAXED
CARDS *Rose-
scented wax scents
and protects the
pressed flowers
on these cards.*

❀ BOOKMARKS *Woodruff decorates and scents the bookmark on the right, that on the left has a spicy clove perfume.*

❀ GIFT TAGS *These tags are perfect for a special gift.*

❀ NOTEPAPER & ENVELOPES *Make matching writing paper, using one or two pressed flowers. Sandalwood perfumes this paper.*

✿ COPPER JUG *Meadowsweet, fennel, soapwort, bergamot, smallage, astrantia, double chamomile, verbena, feverfew and* Inula hookeri *combine to create a striking arrangement in this bright copper jug (below left).*

✿ BRASS KETTLE *Containing stems of euphorbia, lemon balm, vervain, good King Henry, garden rue, lad's love, St John's wort, royal fern and purple sage, this brass kettle (below) is a charming vessel for such a display.*

❧ BOLD DISPLAYS ❧

BOLD BUT SIMPLE SHAPES look stunning in the kitchen whether displayed singly or in groups, on the windowsill, the dresser or even the kitchen table. You can make a wonderful, self-contained decoration with just a few basic, kitchen-related elements. Alternatively, by using a wealth of plant material of many different hues, you can build up a tremendously exuberant and eye-catching display. Designs for the kitchen should always be bright and cheerful so the best colours to use are shades of orange, red, yellow and green. The most suitable scents for these displays are strong, but clean and crisp, and, once again, associated with the kitchen. Spicy or fruity fragrances, for example, will blend in with cooking smells and refresh the kitchen when preparations for the meal are complete.

❀ CITRUS POMANDERS
Oranges, lemons and grapefruit pierced with cloves exude a refreshing and tangy scent. Ribbons, beads and several undecorated fruits complete the arrangement.

❊ VETIVER BELL
Made of vetiver,
which has a persistent,
sweet aroma, this bell is
filled with a beautiful display
of dried plant materials,
including achillea, fir cones, roses,
Doronicum and mosses. The
nutmeg and cinnamon sticks relate
the design to the kitchen and the warm
colours ensure the arrangement is eye-catching.

❧ BURNING PERFUME ❧

ANDLES IN THE KITCHEN evoke a nostalgic, rustic atmosphere. Eating by their mellow light transforms any meal into a special occasion, and the atmosphere is made more memorable if the candles are scented. Candles in the kitchen can be perfumed with herbs, oils and essences, or perhaps the unique, honeyed fragrance of beeswax is the most appealing. Single candles are lovely displayed in traditional holders or on saucers, although table candelabras, holding several tapering candles, will provide more light. An intriguing mixture of perfumes is produced by grouping an assortment of tiny, fragrant candles on a plate. Night lights can be placed in a perfume vaporizer where they will produce a muted light and a strong scent as the perfume evaporates.

❀ MATCHING HERB CANDLES
These candles are all decorated with old-fashioned, cottage-garden herbs. They are scented with lemon balm, thyme, rosemary and bergamot.

❀ HEART-SHAPED CANDLE
This peppermint-scented candle (left) is decorated with borage.

❀ DAINTY CANDLES *Tiny candles (left) are pretty when clustered on a plate.*

❀ BAYBERRY
CANDLES *These
simple and pleasing
candles are scented
with bayberry essence.*

❀ BEESWAX
CANDLES *The rich,
honeyed scent of
these candles adds
to their charm.*

❀ PERFUME VAPORIZER
*The bowl of perfume is placed
above the lighted candle and the heat
from the candle causes the perfume to
evaporate, so creating a pervading aroma.*

THE DINING ROOM

WHETHER YOU HAVE a dining room that is elegant and sophisticated or informal and cottagey, you can perfume it in many delightful ways. Like the banqueting halls of ages past, you can strew the floors with sweet-smelling herbs, although the concept might prove a little overwhelming in the smaller rooms of this day and age! A better idea may be to recreate the pot pourris of our ancestors by gathering the same materials from the garden as they did, mixing them with spices and finally adding the precious essential oils. Make sure that the fragrance is not too strong, so that the appetising aromas of the food can be savoured. The soft and gentle perfumes of lavender, roses, heliotrope, geranium and lemon verbena are perfect as they remain in the background and only manifest their fragrance

❀ SCENTED LINEN *Napkins (above) and tablecloths are imbued with gentle fragrances by storing them with scented sachets in a linen press (left) or dresser.*

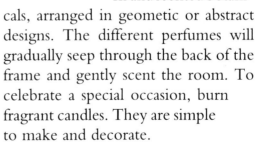

when there is no other to compete with. Create pretty, perfumed sachets and cushions that reflect the colours of your dining room or an intricate and sumptuous table centrepiece. Look for inspiration for designs in decorative china, embroidery and even fragile lace doilies. Make the most of the subtle colours and fascinating textures of dried botanicals. Arrange tiny bouquets to adorn napkin rings or place settings or large displays to loop over chair backs, all redolent with gentle perfumes. Design deep-framed collages using a variety of pot pourris and scented botanicals, arranged in geometic or abstract designs. The different perfumes will gradually seep through the back of the frame and gently scent the room. To celebrate a special occasion, burn fragrant candles. They are simple to make and decorate.

❀ RED WINE *Wine has a pleasing bouquet, which adds to the ambience of an evening meal.*

❀ POPPYSEED ROLL *Fresh bread has a wonderfully appetising aroma.*

❧ TABLE DECOR ❧

SCENTED DECORATIONS for the dining-room table make an important dinner party or romantic evening meal even more special. Matching posies for each place setting are very effective. Alternatively, if you feel adventurous, a floral centrepiece of dried flowers looks stunning. If you also perfume the napkins and tablecloth, ensure that the fragrance of the floral decorations complements them.

✿ FLORAL CENTREPIECE
Beautifully made with rose buds, roses, globe amaranths, sea carrot and larkspur, this flower-scented decoration (above) looks perfect placed in the centre of the dining table.

✿ LILAC NAPKIN
Store delicately scented sachets with napkins and tablecloths to imbue them with a gentle perfume.

137

❧ AROMATIC FOOD ❧

THERE ARE many plant materials that can be used to enhance the appearance, flavour and fragrance of food. Herbs and spices are reknowned for their flavoursome properties; less well known is that flowers can be used in a similar way. The lovely shapes and colours of flowers make them ideal for decorating sweet dishes and their scent adds a delicate flavour. Try making everyday foods, such as butter and sugar, more exciting by garnishing and flavouring them with flowers, and decorate cakes and chocolates with crystallized flowers.

❀ ROSE-PETAL JAM
Rose-petal jam is delicately flavoured and has a gentle perfume.

❀ FLORAL
CHOCOLATES
Mint chocolates decorated with crystallized flowers are a lovely gift.

❀ FLOWER BUTTER
Violets, lavender and sweet Cicely leaves decorate this butter.

❀ SCENTED SUGAR
Store a vanilla pod and lavender with sugar to make a scented sweetener.

❀ ELDERFLOWER CHAMPAGNE
Elderflowers make a wonderful, fragrant, fizzy champagne.

❀ FLOWER CAKE
This beautiful moist sponge cake is decorated with crystallized flowers for a teatime treat.

139

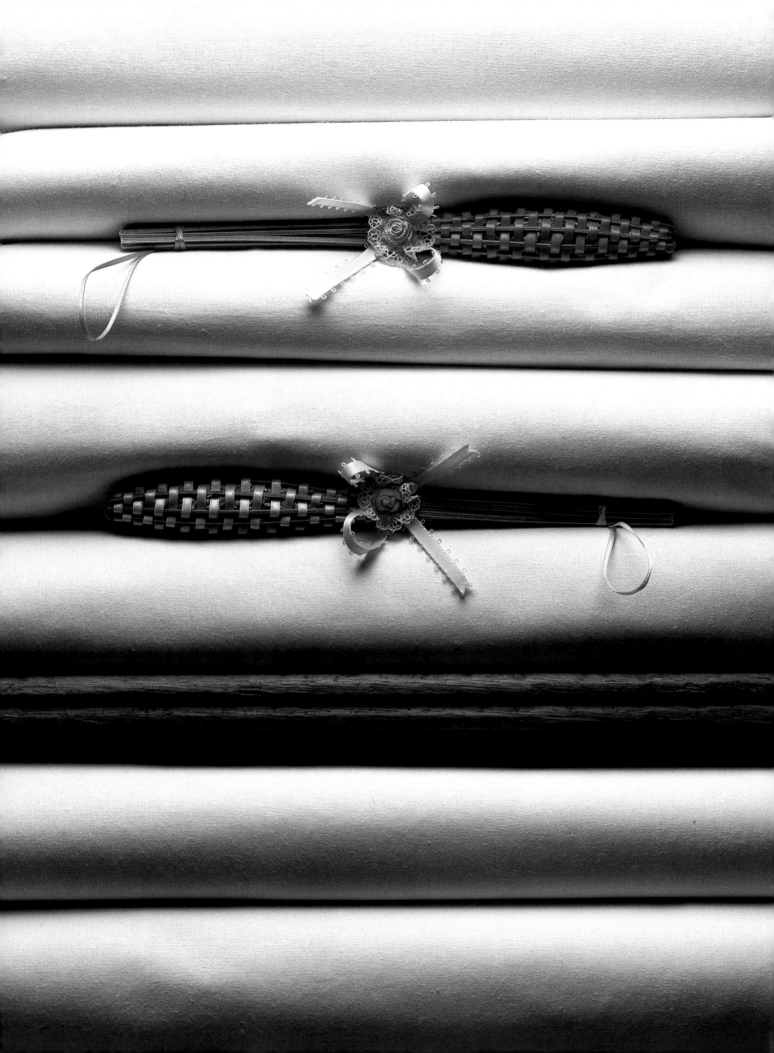

The Bedroom

❋

Whatever the style of your bedroom – intimate and Victorian, stark and modern, or traditional and chintzy – you can make it redolent with complementary perfumes. An ideal pot pourri for the bedroom is the lovely rose, lavender and carnation mix, which you can sharpen by adding peppermint, orange or lemon. Fill pillows with soothing pot pourris. Try stuffing a large pillow with a hop, lemon and lavender mix – recommended by George III as an excellent sleep inducer. Another traditional filler for pillows is a mixture of woodruff and agrimony leaves. The coumarin contained in them becomes more fragrant with age. Old, white lacy pillows, cushions and nightdress cases, beloved of the Victorians, look delightful in almost any bedroom, as do little antique lace sachets, although you can use any fabric

❋ Scented Delights *The exquisite lavender bundles (left) and the delicate sachets (above) are ideal for scenting clothes and linen.*

you like. Fill sachets with much stronger mixes than pillows. Make these soft and floral, hot and spicy, herby or even camphorous. Pop little moth repellant sachets in drawers and hang them in wardrobes. Drawer liners can also be scented with a moth repellant mix, or you can try a floral one if you prefer. Floral pomanders are lovely and a little unusual, or try making simple citrus pomanders – men often prefer the hot fragrance. Unglazed lidded pots will diffuse perfume into the room. Just drop a little essential oil into the pot before filling it with a very strong pot pourri – marigold is an excellent fragrance to use. Place the pots by the bedside so that the soothing perfume drifts over you as you sleep. Store natural beauty products in old bottles or jars. Arranged on the dressing table they are both useful and decorative.

❋

❀ NIGHTDRESS CASE
*(below) Place a scented
sachet, filled with a
favourite mix, in your
nightdress case.*

❀ SCATTER CUSHIONS
*Scented with a gentle and
soothing pot pourri, these
lovely lacy pillows (above
and below) produce a
beautiful subtle fragrance
and are an attractive
decoration for the bedroom.*

142

❧ SATIN & WHITE LACE ❧

PILLOWS FOR THE BEDROOM can be filled with soothing herbal mixes or light, floral pot pourris. Arranged on the bed, they will perfume the whole room as well as scenting the bedlinen. Try filling the pillows with a mix containing hops – traditionally held to be a relaxant – and the gentle fragrance will help you to sleep. White pillow cases embroidered or covered with lace look lovely in any bedroom as their traditional designs complement most decorations. If you prefer to have patterned pillow-cases, use muted colours to complement relaxing fragrances, and bright colours to accentuate more pervasive perfumes.

❀ SLEEP PILLOW
Filled with a soothing mix, largely of hops but with a hint of lavender, this pillow is beneficial for all those who have trouble sleeping.

❧ CREAMS, FLORAL WATERS & COLOGNES ❧

PERFUMES AND COSMETICS are simple to make at home and, as well as being natural, they are a wonderful addition to the scent and decoration of the bedroom. Flowers, herbs and essential oils are used to perfume home-made cosmetics. The scent you choose is a matter of personal preference, although some plants, such as elderflowers and chamomile, are particularly suitable for making creams and oils as they possess soothing and cleansing properties. Choose attractive bottles, jars and pots for your perfumes and cosmetics, and decorate them with ribbons and pressed flowers.

❀ HONEYSUCKLE CREAM *This deliciously fragrant honeysuckle cream (right) is perfect for soothing areas of dry skin and for use as a body lotion.*

❀ JONQUILS *Fresh, highly scented jonquils are lovely in the bedroom.*

❀ ELDERFLOWER CREAM *Elderflower cream (left) has a refreshing fragrance and can be used as a nourishing and toning cream for the face and body.*

❀ FLORAL COLOGNES
Sweet-scented flowers can be used to produce lovely colognes. These bottles (far left) contain jonquil cologne (see p.120) and violet and heliotrope cologne.

❀ ROSE WATER & BODY OIL
The dark blue bottle (far right) contains rose water – a sweet-scented perfume. Body oil (right), made with almond oil and any essential oil, (see p.120) is perfect for softening the skin.

❀ FRAGRANT TALCUM POWDER
A few drops of a favourite essential oil transforms unscented talc into something special.

❀ HAND CREAM *This hand cream is scented with a few drops of essential oil.*

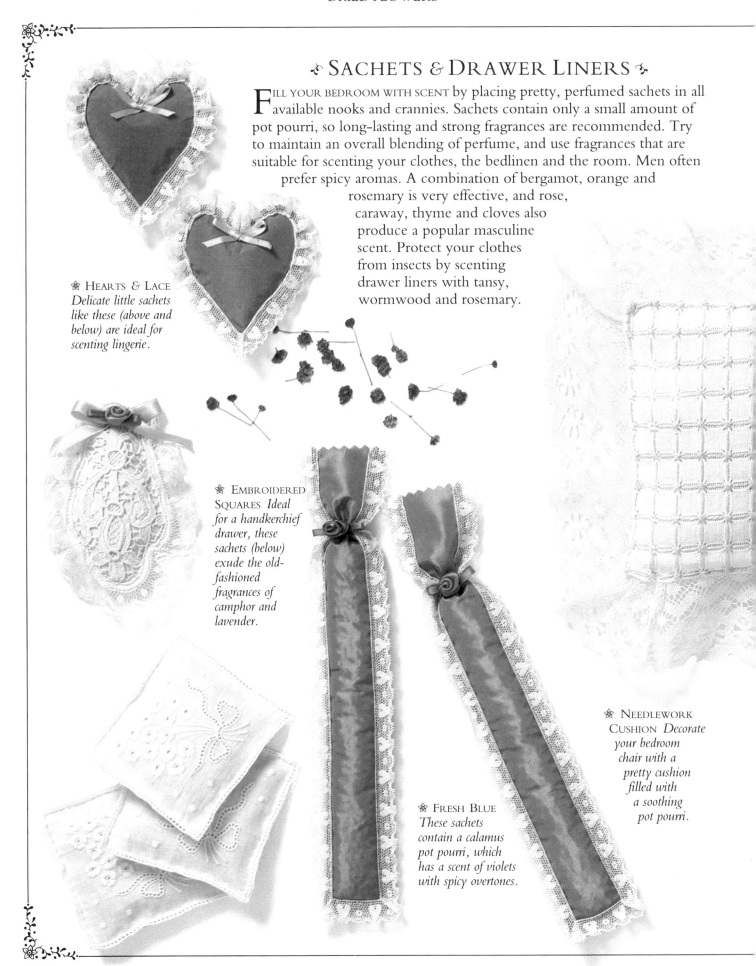

❧ SACHETS & DRAWER LINERS ❧

FILL YOUR BEDROOM WITH SCENT by placing pretty, perfumed sachets in all available nooks and crannies. Sachets contain only a small amount of pot pourri, so long-lasting and strong fragrances are recommended. Try to maintain an overall blending of perfume, and use fragrances that are suitable for scenting your clothes, the bedlinen and the room. Men often prefer spicy aromas. A combination of bergamot, orange and rosemary is very effective, and rose, caraway, thyme and cloves also produce a popular masculine scent. Protect your clothes from insects by scenting drawer liners with tansy, wormwood and rosemary.

❀ HEARTS & LACE
Delicate little sachets like these (above and below) are ideal for scenting lingerie.

❀ EMBROIDERED SQUARES *Ideal for a handkerchief drawer, these sachets (below) exude the old-fashioned fragrances of camphor and lavender.*

❀ NEEDLEWORK CUSHION *Decorate your bedroom chair with a pretty cushion filled with a soothing pot pourri.*

❀ FRESH BLUE
These sachets contain a calamus pot pourri, which has a scent of violets with spicy overtones.

❀ DRAWER LINERS
*Line your drawers
with perfumed paper
to ensure that your
clothes are always
sweetly scented.*

❀ DAINTY LACE
*Round or square,
lace sachets are
perfect for placing
among clothes
and bedlinen.*

THE NURSERY

THERE IS NO BETTER WAY to encourage a love of the natural world in your child than by taking him or her into the garden to gather herbs and flowers that will ultimately be used to fill toys. Your child will remember plant names and fragrances with enthusiasm, and will love to be involved in making the toys. There are many playthings you can make that can also be scented. Simply adapt any ideas you have to include either a pot pourri stuffing or a scented sachet. For example, dolls full of lavender, herb-stuffed teddies and a curious Suffolk puff caterpillar, which is made of patchwork circles each filled with a different mix. Nothing could be more exciting to a child than an array of fragrances. In the nineteenth century it was recommended that nurseries were scented with the spicy aromas of cloves, nutmeg, cinnamon and caraway. However, children soon discover their own favourite scents. These often relate to the familiar smell of the kitchen – orange and lemon, and peppermint and spearmint are all popular. These fresh aromas are ideal for the nursery because they are also quite soothing; add one or two of them, together with a little lavender, to a hop-stuffed cushion and you will have a traditional "sleep pillow". Hot-water-bottle covers or nightdress cases are easily made and can be perfumed by tucking a sachet inside the case or into a pocket sewn on the front. Sachets can range from rose-scented dolls to tiny lavender teddies and from little herby chicks to simple spicy squares. Bright colours are beloved of children and look delightful in the nursery. Of course, there are some children who prefer subdued colours and more sophisticated perfumes. So work with them when scenting and decorating their rooms.

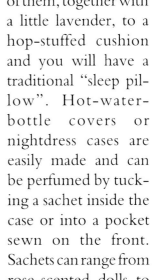

❀ FRAGRANT TOYS & PILLOWS
Brighten and perfume the nursery by making scented toys (above) or fill pillows with fragrant mixes (left).

❀❀ NOT ALL THE TOYS SHOWN HERE ARE SUITABLE FOR PLAYING WITH, AND CARE SHOULD BE TAKEN TO DISPLAY THEM OUT OF THE REACH OF VERY YOUNG CHILDREN.

❀ GREEN TEDDY *Made from nylon lace and filled with a lemon-scented mix, this teddy is only suitable for decorative purposes.*

❀ SLEEP TEDDY *This teddy is filled with a soothing peppermint and hop mixture. Hang him out of reach over the bed or cot.*

❀ TEDDIES & CHICKS *Made to match the bigger toys, these herb-scented sachets can be tucked between clothes or bedlinen.*

❀ MOTHER HEN *Filled with a herby mix, this colourful hen looks lovely when displayed with her two yellow chicks.*

❧ AROMATIC TOYS ❧

AROMATIC SOFT TOYS add a new dimension to the nursery. Hang a lavender doll in the nursery and the scent of lavender will fill the room. Teddy and chicken sachets are simple to make and they, too, will gently perfume the air; alternatively, tucked into drawers they will sweeten the contents. If you are making toys for very young children, encase the pot pourri in fire-resistant wadding to make them safe to play with, or display them out of reach.

❀ FLORAL DOLLS *Easily made from tiny scraps of material and filled with rose petals, these sachet dolls are perfect for putting in chests of drawers and cupboards.*

❀ DAINTY DOLLS *Embroidered faces, lace and ribbons transform these simple sachets into lovely dolls.*

❀ LAVENDER LILY *This enchanting doll is made with net material and filled with lavender. She is the ideal decoration for a little girl's nursery and will imbue the room with the fragrance of lavender.*

❀ HOT-WATER-BOTTLE
COVER *A simple and useful
bedtime accessory, this hot-
water-bottle cover is scented
with sachets placed in
the little front pocket.*

❀ TEDDIES
*These sachets are
ideal for providing
a gentle perfume.
Fill each teddy
with a different
mix to vary
the fragrance
as desired.*

❀ GINGHAM
PYJAMA CASE *A
lovely pyjama case
brightens the cot
during the day
and scents the
nightwear kept
inside it.*

❧ TIME FOR BED ❧

Most children like to be tucked up with a teddy or doll or a comforter of some kind at bedtime. It is often a very simple object that reassures children who are afraid of the dark if they wake in the night. Regular bedtime accessories, such as hot-water-bottle covers, pillows and pyjama cases, are ideal companions, and are easily scented with sachets or by putting pot pourri inside an envelope of stuffing, which is then placed inside the cloth cover.

✿ CO-ORDINATING ACCESSORIES *Made with matching material and filled with complementary pot pourris, this pillow and pyjama case are wonderful additions to the nursery.*

✿ STRAW TOYS
Little straw toys are scented by being placed in a pot pourri or by rubbing them with a little essential oil.

THE BATHROOM

❋

BEAUTIFUL, perfumed pot pourris, pretty bouquets and garlands, baskets of flowers and stunning botanical friezes will transform any bathroom. Shells, sea glass, mosses, lichens, flowers, and silks and satins can all be found in wonderful shades of aquamarine, which, when they are mixed with mauve-blues, produce diffused, underwater colours that are ideal for the bathroom. Create contrasts by adding touches of pink and dark red, or yellow and orange to these hues. Large Abalone shells, with their wonderful, iridescent green linings, make beautiful containers for pot pourris. Decorated with whole flowers and spices they become pretty, textured tapestries. Try filling a large terracotta basket with dried flowers. Add artificially dyed flowers in shades of turquoise, jade and pink to accentuate the colours of the sea. Make substantial and opulent bouquets or tiny nosegays. Embellish garlands with small, scented shells and sea glass, fragrant flowers and even seaweed. Alternatively, adorn your wall with a luxuriant frieze – create a delicate landscape of pressed flowers, mosses and lichens. Use a floral sealer to protect dried-flower arrangements from the steamy atmosphere. Mix floral scents with sharp lemon, pine, geranium and orange to refresh their sweetness. Anise and orange makes an interesting combination, as does rose and orange. On the other hand, you may prefer the sweet oriental perfumes of ylang ylang or exquisite jasmine. Store home-made bath essences, oils, shampoos and toilet vinegars in antique bottles and decorate them with dried flowers and ribbons to add to the overall charm of the bathroom.

❋ BATH LUXURIES *Treat yourself to a fragrant bath (left) by adding rose petals and home-made bath oil to the water and using essential oil soap.*

❋

❧ POSIES & WREATHS ❧

THE SEASIDE is a particularly apt and traditional theme to follow when decorating the bathroom. In your posies and wreaths use colours that are in keeping with the seaside – turquoise, blue and sea-green are ideal as they evoke clear skies and enticing water. Flowers that have been dyed blue or green will not look out of place, especially if used sparingly to highlight the appearance of the mix. Add shells and pebbles to the plant material, to complete the theme. All sorts of scents suit the bathroom and, although the fragrance you choose should not be overpowering, it can be quite strong. Hang posies and wreaths on walls, from the ceiling, on the side of the bath, or on the mirror.

ANAPHALIS
(DYED JADE)

LAVENDER

❀ LARGE POSY *Among the medley of flowers used in this pretty bouquet are everlasting flowers and sea carrot. Rose oil, dropped in the centres of the rose buds, mingles with the perfume of the lavender.*

❀ PETITE POSY *This charming little posy, which matches the seaside wreath in colour, is scented with star anise and orange oil.*

❀ SEA GLASS *These pretty glass fragments were scented by steeping them in a jar of perfumed essence.*

156

ANAPHALIS
(DYED PINK)

ROSE

❀ SEASIDE WREATH *This
wreath is scented with lemon and
bergamot oils and is reminiscent
of the seaside in its display of
shells and colours such as sea-
green, cream and turquoise.*

❀ FORMAL CIRCLET
*The scent of roses and
geranium oil pervades
this circlet of red roses
and pink- and jade-
dyed anaphalis.*

SEA CARROT

STATICE

157

❀ BUBBLE BATHS
*Floral or spicy
perfumes can be
used to make
luxurious
bubble baths.*

❧ SOAPS & SHAMPOOS ❧

SPECIAL SOAPS and shampoos, bath oils, bubble baths
and toilet vinegars are lovely to have in the
bathroom. All these toiletries are simple to make
at home and can be scented with your favourite
fragrances. Decorate the bottles with dried flowers
and pretty ribbons, and they will look lovely
arranged on the shelves and around the bath.

❋ TOILET VINEGAR
*Geranium leaves and
oakmoss scent this
toilet vinegar (far right).*

❋ HAIR RINSE *After
shampooing, a chamomile
hair rinse (centre) is perfect
for reviving the hair.*

❋ BATH OIL
*(right) This
relaxing bath
oil is scented
with orange
and rose
essential oils.*

Rosa

❋ DRY SHAMPOO *Scented
with rosemary, this dry
shampoo (left) quickly
refreshes your hair.*

❋ BATH BAGS *Filled with
dried herbs, these sachets
(above) will make your bath
water scented and refreshing.*

❋ ESSENTIAL OIL SOAP
*These soaps are lovely
for guests or for your
own personal use.*

✧ CONSERVATION OF WILD PLANTS ✧

THROUGH MY LOVE of gardening and my interest in the historical significance of our wild and cultivated plants, has grown an awareness of the threat that we pose to the survival of our environment. There must now be some redress to the balance of the intricate and fragile equilibrium of the natural world. Everyone can make some contribution towards this and I hope that the contents of this book will encourage all those who read it to experiment with alternative ways of freshening and sweetening their homes. I also hope that it will stimulate an interest in natural beauty preparations. All these fragrant delights are bio-degradable and pose no threat to the atmosphere.

Most of the wild and cultivated plants that I use in my recipes are grown and gathered from my own garden. In my tamed wilderness, wildlings grow cheek by jowl with their cultivated cousins and the garden is a haven for the prolific Cornish wildlife. Help to protect the environment by trying to grow wild species in your garden – many seed merchants sell wild plant seed and there are specialist nurseries from whom you can buy wild plants.

If you do gather wild flowers never pick them from a plant that has no companions, always leave some flowers to set seed and never pick more flowers than you need. I believe that we should all grow some wild plants in our gardens for by so doing we can at least ensure their perpetuation. Many wild plants are now protected and should under no circumstances be touched. A list of these is available from Department of the Environment, Tollgate House, Houlton Street, Bristol BS2 9DJ.

✧ POISONOUS PLANTS ✧

TAKE GREAT CARE in gathering plants, flowers, berries and seeds. Often, those that appear to be the brightest and most attractive are, in fact, poisonous. The following is a list of the more common poisonous berries. Do **not** use them in your preparations. No matter how beautiful they are, it is not worth the risk.

Common Name	Latin Name	Common Name	Latin Name
Black Locust	*Robinia pseudoacacia*	Mayapple, mandrake	*Podophyllum peltatum*
Castor-bean	*Ricinus communis*	Poison ivy	*Rhus radicans*
Common moonseed	*Menispermum canadense*	Poison sumac	*Rhus vernix*
Deadly nightshade	*Solanum dulcamara*	Pokeweed	*Phytolacca americana*
English ivy	*Hedera helix*	Spindle tree	*Euonymus europaea*
February daphne	*Daphne mezereum*	Wisteria	*Wisteria* spp.
Golden-chain	*Laburnum anagyroides*	Yews	*Taxus* spp.